THE
CENTURY
SPEAKS

voices of
WORCESTERSHIRE

Derrick Bollen marries Connie at Tibberton church in 1941.

THE CENTURY SPEAKS
voices of WORCESTERSHIRE

Memories of Worcestershire people
compiled by Genevieve Tudor from interviews by Julia Letts and Sue Broome
for the **BBC Hereford and Worcester** *series*
The Century Speaks

TEMPUS

First published 1999
Copyright © BBC Hereford and Worcester, 1999

Tempus Publishing Limited
The Mill, Brimscombe Port,
Stroud, Gloucestershire, GL5 2QG

ISBN 0 7524 1837 8

Typesetting and origination by
Tempus Publishing Limited
Printed in Great Britain by
Midway Clark Printing, Wiltshire

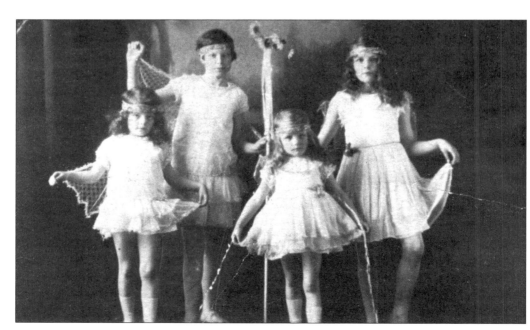

Once a dancer … Tony Baxter, aged four.

CONTENTS

Foreword   6

1. Where we live   9
2. House and home   19
3. Who are we?   31
4. Money and the workplace   38
5. Living together   48
6. Crime and the law   60
7. Growing up and getting older   68
8. Technology   81
9. Food   91
10. Playtime   98
11. Going places   107
12. Life and death   115
13. Beliefs and fears   123

Winifred and Nellie Barber with their bikes in 1931.

FOREWORD

This is my chance to say a huge thank you to all those who agreed to tell me their stories for *The Century Speaks*. It took me the best part of six months to record the interviews (many of which are reproduced in this book) and every minute of it was a privilege and a pleasure.

Each interview has been unique and I've been amazed by people's honesty and the clarity of their memories; for example, a ninety-year-old woman's vivid description of seeing one of the first moving pictures, a man of nearly seventy re-living his experience of being 'birched' at Worcester police station, and a fascinating description of life on the barges from an eighty-year-old man who still lives by the canal at Alvechurch.

I've discovered corners of Worcestershire that I didn't know existed and I've gained an extraordinary insight into the lives of about a hundred people from the county. Many interviewees told me things that they had never told anyone before. Often we cried together.

And of course there have been plenty of laughs. In amongst the extracts in this book, you'll find the story of a Kidderminster woman who couldn't understand why

Cedric Olive, cider maker, pictured with a sample of the cider apples at Bulmers.

she was the centre of attention at a '50s RAF bop until she realised she'd forgotten to put her knickers on. And then there's the local entertainer who was singing 'Bless This House' in a Worcestershire village hall when the floor caved in beneath him.

Inevitably, in making the radio programmes and compiling this book, we've had to leave tons of material out. This is just a snapshot of the century. If you want the full picture, then go to the British Library and immerse yourself in oral history for a day. Every word we recorded is now part of a new sound archive, 'The Millennium Memory Bank'.

If I have learnt anything from the wonderful people of Worcestershire who have shared their lives with me during this project, it is that we should all do more listening. We should find more time to question and share the experiences of our parents and grandparents, friends and neighbours. Think what a waste it is if we don't.

Julia Letts
Producer

Lilly Peach and 'Johnny Onions' the onion seller are pictured in 1948.

CHAPTER 1
Where we live

The Almonry, in Pershore.

*Perhaps the most evocative way to start a chapter on where we live
is with a poem by Mike Edwards:*

There was a time my children
Before this village grew
When everyone who lived here
Was everyone you knew

There was a time my children
Which seemed so long ago
When all the village taught you
Was all you need to know

The daily round of school life
Then home to work or play
And planning boyish mischief
For the coming Saturday

When grandfathers and fathers
Where thought brother to the ox
The children that they fathered
Were more brothers to the fox

We roamed the fields and hedgerows
We wandered far and wide
Returning when the owl called
Or when the vixen cried

How tall the elm trees grew then
Like stairways to the sky
When sat amongst their branches
You dreamt that you could fly

There was a time my children
But now these times grow few
When the countryside around you
Taught you everything you knew

Mike Edwards, born 1931

From glow-worms and blossom trails to the local variation on Colditz. The villages and towns of Worcestershire itself are seen through the eyes of the people who live here:

I suppose there were about 350 people lived in the village of Cleeve Prior, and some days if it was raining we'd be sat in front of the grate and we'd got fed up of looking for pictures in the fire, the glowing embers. 'What shall we do now?' 'Let's go all through the village and name the people.' We could! You could put a name to all of them and say who they were related to. People had only got to do one or two silly things in their life and it stayed in the village memory and they became known by that. There was Albert Anchors – one of the things he did was the village sexton. He was also the fellow who came along with his wheelbarrow and raked out the earth closets which were at the back of the school. He had some of the best plums anywhere in the allotments that were round the back of the school at that time! And then there was Fred. Fred was the handyman of the village. He could divine water. He could mend shoes and taps. In fact, you could ask Fred to do most jobs – he would get on and do them. Then there was John Montford, a fearsome-looking character, and he used to sit on the village green outside his house in one of these fold-up chairs and I'd go down, 'Morning Mr Montford,' 'Morning Master Edwards.' And I'd walk in a wide circle all the way round, never take my eyes of him, till I'd got round.

Mike Edwards, born 1931

I can remember, stood on the hill, eleven o'clock at night and there were all glow-worms glowing around our feet, and we were thinking about these glow-worms ... and a nightingale started up singing and it was wonderful to stand there and listen to this nightingale. Other things like the red squirrels – I remember the last red squirrel I saw and I think it was in the late '40s and ... I saw it playing in this tree and watching it for ages and I was so sorry they are not about now. The rabbits were another thing. Rabbits were a real pest until the myxomatosis came round. Some of these fields, all round the top, perhaps an acre or two acres would be eaten off with rabbits ... although during the war they were wonderful food. I remember seeing Ernie with a push-bike, so many rabbits on this push-bike – all down the handlebars, all down the crossbar, tied on the back, and he was pushing it back to Clifton, I think. I guessed he'd got fifty pair of rabbits on this push-bike but they used to queue for these rabbits in Birmingham. They were so pleased to have them.

John Thacker, born 1927

Iain Patton was brought up in Northern Ireland but he has made Worcestershire his home:

Living in the Malvern Hills is just superb, looking over Herefordshire and the Welsh Borders and the Severn Valley. We are right at the bottom of the valley by the River Teme and the woodlands round here are superb, much better even than in Ireland. Here the oaks, the broad-leaved woods, that you

11

Chris Cookson is pictured in the Wyre Forest.

have are so superb, the mistletoe draped over every apple tree. It's a beautiful county. You can go to many corners of Worcestershire and sense nothing has changed. Of course things have, but there are remnants of various farms that have been there. You can go into some woods and they are just so rich with mosses, lichens and mistletoe that there's just a timelessness about it, the bluebells which have been there for hundreds of years. I recognise that our landscape has been influenced by people, by farming, by communities so obviously there are changes, but there are many corners, by woodland, by streams, which have been that way for a long time – and long may it continue.

Iain Patton, born 1966

John Robinson has worked in the Wyre Forest for over twenty-one years. He describes the changes:

I'd always had this love of woodland – fresh water and woodland – and I heard on the grapevine this job in the Wyre Forest was coming up. I rang the chief warden up before the job was advertised and I came out here. This house was derelict, nothing here but just a field and we went for a little walk around the reserve and that was it. I got it! That was twenty years ago! Wyre Forest in the Middle Ages stretched from Bridgnorth to Malvern and, originally, and after the last ice age, would be part of the forest that covered 60 million acres of the British Isles. So, it had been drastically reduced down from the Middle Ages down to about 6,000 acres. Since then, there has been

Chris Cookson, aged two, embarks on the *SS Orion* for Australia.

a tremendous amount of management ... it [had] become very sterile, very species monotonous, so my job was to try to get it back to more natural woodland. We actually succeeded. If you go round now, you can find trees one year old, trees two hundred years old, and everything in between.

John Robinson, born 1939

Market days are no longer the same:

The market days would be used as a complete relaxation from the farm. It was where they'd come and sell the stock – where they'd meet people. If you wanted to order your feed or fertilizer ... [it was] ordered on the market day. That had probably gone on for probably 150 years. Tenbury was a very big market, a very big fruit market, a very big sheep and cattle market – and also the famous

Chris Cookson at his home in Australia.

The High Street in Pershore, 1999.

The Monastic Bridge, Pershore.

holly and mistletoe sales, which were unique. It would be quite common to sell 200 tons of plums and damsons in the season on one day. These would go all over the country. The majority seemed to go up north as Evesham seemed to supply the south. Thousands and thousands of eggs, live chickens, live geese, live ducks – all would be bundled into carts, onto trains. Sheep and cattle would be taken by train. It had to change really. It has changed dramatically. The market now on a Tuesday is non existent – a few special sales for stock. This I think eventually will go completely. I think stock will be purchased from the farm by the big companies. Market towns will just be in name and that's all.

Jim Franklin, born 1940

There were two markets in Pershore, the Central Market and the Co-operative Market in Defford Road. The Co-op Market was the bigger one and all the produce from local farms was taken there for sale – and there were still a lot of horses and carts in those days – so there was a long trail of horses and carts, the old original Fordson tractors. There were one or two lorries but it was mainly horse drawn and tractor drawn. They used to queue all along Broad Street and down Bridge Street, waiting for their turn. One of the advantages of the horses was the farmer or the chap could go round to the market and the horse would come round in the queue, all in his own good time. The most common fruit in the area was apples and plums and a few pears. Those were the only fruits available to you in season, of course.

John Hemmings, born 1931

The waterways were used for distribution:

I've gone up from Gloucester, we've hit the ice at Worcester and if it ain't too bad, up to an inch, with a motorboat you could break it. We used to break it with a load, then you'd get your butty [boat] and you'd tow it in. When you got to Birmingham we emptied, and it was the last week before Christmas – I always remembered it. I said to the gaffer, 'We've got to get home for Christmas'. We only had four days left. 'Well,' he said, 'Get on with it'. There were six of us, three motor and three horse boats, and we started off down the canal. We got to Tardebigge – I was the first, went down the locks, got them down into the five-mile pound at Droitwich. I said, 'This is it, we've hit the salt water now' because salt ice don't break like fresh-water ice, it's not brittle. So I said, 'What will we do now? We can't wait for the ice boat to come up to free us, he'll be two days!' So we put three horses on the motor [boat]. We took the three horses off the horse boats and we put them on my motor boat and it took us five hours to do five miles. We pulled her out of the water several times and we had to cut the ice back from round her to put her back in the water again to start again. And that was how we got her out of five-mile pound. I got down to the top of Gilberts and we couldn't go any farther, so the lock-keeper phoned Worcester up and said, 'We've got six of them here. You'll have to send the ice boat up to relieve them'. So, they bought the ice boat up to us at twelve o'clock the next day – they had four horses on the ice boat and it was only a little boat they were

Max Sinclair is seen aboard the *Vesta*.

pulling through it. By the time it got up to us, it was all freezing up again down below. Anyway we got up to Worcester that night, with a bit of pushing and shoving, and the next day we were down on the river and that's the one time I've seen the River Severn froze, 1936 or '37. We got home for Christmas Eve and when I got home I cut the boat in half. The ice, pulling it through the ice, cut all the wood away, right down to the pins. I had to go up to the dry dock after Christmas. I took twelve tons of barley up to the vinegar brewery in Stourport and I put her in dry dock there.

Tom Mayo, born 1916

Sometimes the town planners don't always get it right:

Of course, there's a classic little story in Pershore, you know. A very old part of the town was demolished completely and a new site existed and was developed, and the houses, I believe, are very nice to live in and very comfortable. But they are unusual elevations, all sort of different elevations and levels. Nonetheless for that, it did win a national architectural award but the council was aghast when the locals christened it 'Colditz'. And that's still the name applied to that estate to this day in Pershore, and even postmen have had letters addressed 'Mr. So-and-So, number so-and-so, Colditz, Pershore!'

John Hemming, born 1931

Bewdley is everything to me. I can't tell you how my heart lifts up when I come back. When I first bought the house, when I drove towards it, I'd bought it in November so it was Christmas time. When you see the lights over the water it was just fantastic. It's beautiful to look at and that's what brought me here initially but it isn't just that. It's the people. The first night I came here, I'd been teaching at college and I had the keys to the house that day, and I knew that I'd got to come and have a look at it, and it was about nine o'clock and I was scared to death. I opened the front door and there was an envelope on the mat and I thought, 'Good grief, here's my first bill!' And I lifted it up and it was a card that said,

Max Sinclair aboard the *Vesta*.

Astwood Farm, surrounded by snow.

'Welcome to your new home. We hope you'll be really happy next door to us – Jane and Dave and Tom and Joey'. And that was an indication of what it's like here. That Christmas, I had loads of Christmas cards. All the people sent me a card and put their name and number of where they lived – so Bewdley has welcomed me. There's a really caring atmosphere here.

Cynthia Pearson, born 1938

Jean Nichols sums up her feeling for the county she lives in:

What I love about Worcestershire is that I think of it as a heart. It always reminds me of a little heart. We're quite central to everything and we've got all the beautiful countryside around, which I adore. All the lovely walks, all the beautiful scenery. But you've also got all the history attached. You've got Worcester and the cathedral and you've got Bewdley, steeped in history, with Henry the Eighth that went there and stayed there. You've got Droitwich being a spa town, you've got the Malverns – one mustn't forget the Malverns – they are so beautiful! You can get all the presence of Elgar and you imagine him riding across the top of the Malverns. But the place that I live at the moment is very, very special. It is so beautiful. It is in the country and out of all the places in Worcestershire it is my Shangri-La.

Jean Nichols, born 1940

CHAPTER 2

House and home

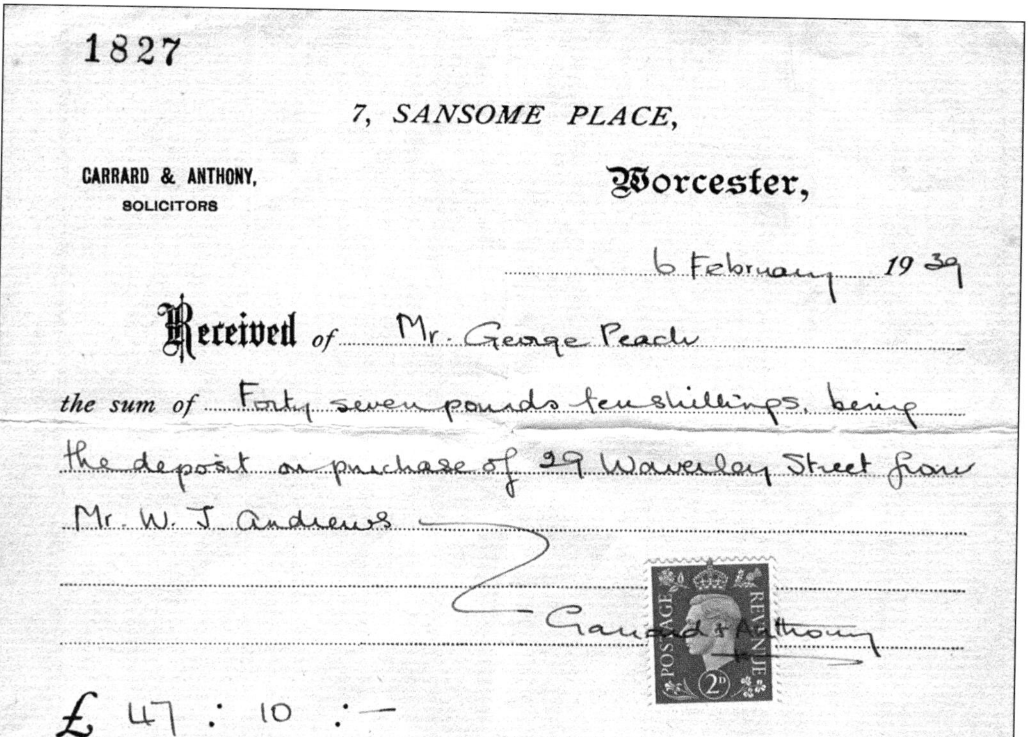

1827

7, SANSOME PLACE,

CARRARD & ANTHONY,
SOLICITORS

Worcester,

6 February 1939

Received *of* Mr. George Peach

the sum of Forty seven pounds ten shillings, being the deposit on purchase of 29 Waverley Street from Mr. W. J. Andrews

Garrard & Anthony

£ 47 : 10 : —

This house purchase receipt dates from 1939.

The outside loo and the communal tap in the backyard come under close scrutiny. There are stories of coloured bathroom suites and avant-garde lamps, the two-up and two-down and the manor house, the horse-drawn wagon and the narrow boat. Worcestershire people invite us in for a closer look at their homes:

The house I lived in was an old house, half timbered. It was very comfortable but of course it was very primitive. Inside the house were flagstone floors, very low ceilings, few cupboards and a great big black range in the kitchen for cooking. There was a sitting room, very small, which was quite comfortable. [There was] a nice open fire. There was no water, no electric light – all oil lamps and candles. There was an outside toilet up the garden, no toilet rolls those days. We used to tear paper up into squares, put a piece of string through it and hang it in the loo. It was a bucket job underneath!

Ellis Wilson, born 1907

It wasn't until 1949 we had electricity. We did improve on our lighting a bit because the Fountain Inn, below in the village, converted to Calor gas and we had all their lamps distributed around the village. They were a well-known make, they were Aladdin and they had a mantle on and they gave a brilliant light and I thought, 'By God, we've moved into the twentieth century!'

Ron Jennings, born 1927

Harriet Hall lived in a horse-drawn caravan when she was a girl:

We always used to carry a dry toilet. It was a bucket you could put a

The Land Oak public house.

Kemises House, Cleeve Prior, in the 1930s.

Mr Bell's family's horse-drawn wagon, 1908.

Kemises Cottage in the 1940s.

sheet in and when you used it, you had to bury it and put a drop of bleach down. When you wanted to do your washing you'd make a big fire outside and you'd lay a big bath across it. That was what you boil your water in. Now, I don't believe in boiling my tea towels in where I done my other washing, my underclothes. I let my daughter take my washing now, but I won't let her take my tea towels. I say, 'You're not going to put my tea towels in with your dirty pants!'

Harriet Hall, born 1922

Outside our house was a tap, nailed to the wall, and it was a communal tap. Everyone in the court used it. The house itself was built of wattle and plaster. It was very fragile. You could push your finger through it, no bricks. We were next door to the Angel Hotel. We had a courtyard at the back, and the courtyard at night was lit up and that provided light for our bedroom. Our bedroom had no glass in the windows. It was just bars. One bed and four children – two at the top and two at the bottom – that's how we used to sleep.

Derrick Bollen, born 1917

You always went to bed with a coat on top of the bed to keep you warm and mum couldn't afford lots of blankets so you just had your sheet and blanket, an eiderdown if you were lucky, but a coat on the top of that. There was a yard and there was a brew house, where your mother stood and did the washing with a huge great mangle. After she'd done the washing she'd say, 'There's some beautiful suds left, come and have a bath'. The tin bath was taken off the wall and you'd have this lovely bath once a week. Because none of the houses had any water in, people needed to come and fill their enamel jugs. It started to get a bit of a pain when you were thirteen, and quite a well-developed young girl, that you'd got the men coming in with their enamel jugs to fill up! [It was] never very warm. There were gaps under the door and you'd roll up a bit of coat, or felt.

Jean Nichols, born 1940

This house has been Winifred Barber's home since 1982.

A narrow boat on its travels in Pershore.

Wash day was a little different then:

In the kitchen there was a copper in the corner, then there was a great big black fire grate with hobs and ovens where you could bake bread. And this boiling copper was filled every week to do the washing … first of all mother'd have the clothes on the sink and well soak them. Anything that was a bit soiled, that was done on the rubbing board with a scrubbing brush and then everything was put into the maiding tub with hot water and this great big wooded maid … there was a handle on the top and a long pole and on the bottom was big pegs, and you'd keep doing it up and down into the washing to get all the dirt out. Those Victorian houses had long gardens. If you went down our garden and looked across all the gardens you could see all the washing blowing in the wind – it was wonderful, but hard work really.

Winifred Barber, born 1907

Margot Beard discovered it was less expensive to move into a large house than a three-bedroomed one:

We lived in a very, very small attractive house in Bromwich Lane. My mother was living with us, we by now had two children. There wasn't room to move – we had to move. We looked at all the three-bedroomed houses that were available. They were all fantastically dear. The only houses that were not dear were the very big houses that nobody wanted. So we moved out to Turret House at Hampton Lovett, which was an enormous Victorian house. It had five acres of land, and kitchens and

laundries and butlers' pantries – you name it we'd got it! But there was room for the children to go wild. There was country all round us and like my own childhood, they were able to run free. There were no restrictions, there were no fears. The house was leasehold, which made it cheaper, and it had a cottage so we had a gardener, and I couldn't have managed the place on my own, I had to have some help so I asked the blacksmith down at the bottom of the hill if he'd send his daughter up to me, and the blacksmith's wife said, 'Oh, you couldn't have Lillian, Mrs Beard. She's the sickly one!' and I said, 'Well, send Lillian up to me for a fortnight and we'll see'. And of course Lillian put on weight as soon as she came to me and Lillian wasn't sickly anymore. After Lillian had been with me for two years her younger sister Daisy arrived. She simply took it for granted she was coming. She said, 'I've come Mrs Beard' and I dressed them in pretty clothes – they had gingham morning dresses and attractive afternoon dresses and they were proud of how they looked, and when we went on holiday we took them with us. We took a big furnished house and we took the girls with us and a girl from the orphanage, so we were a very big family when we went on holiday.

Margot Beard, born 1912

Tony Baxter decided to increase her family so she could live in better conditions:

We got this home when our second daughter was two and a half. I'd been to the council and said, 'Please, is

Tony Baxter's house, March 1950.

there any way you can get a home for me?' I threatened, 'I shall have to live in a tent if not, and take my babies with me'. The council said, 'Are you expecting?' 'No.' 'If you were expecting a third you'd get a house, there's a new batch of houses being built'. These were the first post-war houses. I just went back up and said, 'Right, this is what [they] said. We don't get a house until we're expecting a third baby. How about it?' And that was it! We went for a third baby and we went down to the doctor's two or three weeks later and said, 'I'm pregnant'. We got our names down for a house, and three weeks after that we had the house. I think really it's what I'm accusing a lot of the young girls of today of doing – having your baby to get the house. But at least we had justification that we already had two children

Tony Baxter, born 1909

Tony Baxter's garden in 1963.

25

Moving to England, Yvonne Welsh was determined to own her own home:

We said that from the very day we arrived, 'If we could only buy our own house'. And what happened, as soon as we left for England, my father got up the courage because he knew then he'd have somebody to come to. And they came and stayed with us, and they all got jobs but it didn't work, our two families living together – two young families … When I used to go to work they'd say, 'What's up today?' Then I'd burst into tears and tell them. Then [someone] said to me, 'Do you know they are giving 100% mortgages to buy houses – why don't you go and find out about it?' They told me what bus to catch to get to Stourport and where to go to ask. I went to the treasurers' offices and I said, 'I believe you're giving 100 per cent mortgages' and he said, 'Yes we are but

you'll have to pay a big rent and you've only just come to the country'. I asked how much it would be and he told me the price of the house and he worked it all out. He said, 'Your rent will be £3 10s'. I said, 'I'd been paying five guineas for a whole year so I think I could afford to pay £3 10s'. So he said, 'You've got it all worked out. Here are the forms – fill them in and bring them back as quickly as you can'. So in about three weeks we'd got the 100 per cent to go and choose a house and I went to the estate agents and he showed me a plan of these houses. I didn't know where the area was so I said, 'Which house will be ready?' and he said, 'Number two, number one has already been sold' so I said I'd have number two. That's how I chose my house. We used to come every week to see this house being built!

Yvonne Welsh, born 1929

This is the house where Yvonne Welsh grew up in Secunderabad, India.

Yvonne Welsh's house, No. 2, The Priory.

Iain Patton spent time in a community based in the Malvern Hills. He describes what it was like:

The name of the community is Birchwood Hall. It was one of the first to be set up by a group of people who pooled their money and bought this tumbledown Victorian hall – visually, wonderful. You're on the Malvern Hills, surrounded by woods and by wonderful countryside. It was a very loved place, well-tended gardens. It looked good inside. There are three architects and a designer that live there too and there's obviously quite a bit of creative thought gone into the place ...

people were very warm and very welcoming ... and were entirely normal! Civil servants, a potter, a photographer ... very ordinary people We, to some degree, income shared. You each paid a rent based on what you earned. If you had children they lived there freely and you actually paid less rent. You also had alternating 'business' and 'feelings' meetings. The business meetings were where you get on with the basics of making sure you'd got enough firewood to heat the place, paid the phone bill – and feelings meeting were making sure we were getting on well together, working as a team. Birchwood Hall started twenty-six, twenty-seven years ago, and there's actually one of the original members still there, and it's well established. The place relied very much on your wanting to be there, wanting to be part of that group and to pull your weight, and it worked very well.

Iain Patton, born 1966

Max Sinclair was inspired by a work colleague:

Most people followed the 'trad' [design]. The next office to me, was a chap called Colin Gubbins. He said, 'You and Jocelyn come one evening for supper'. We went to this little red brick house expecting to open the parlour door and see the piano, those sort of things, and we opened the door and we could not believe it. The walls were dark purple with gold stars and the whole thing was magic! We went in and had supper and we had contemporary knives and forks rather than the old-fashioned bone-handled knives and forks, and driving home together we said, 'That's what we want to do!' 'Contemporary' was the term in those days and we had contemporary furniture. I remember my uncle in Birmingham said, 'What can we buy you as a wedding present?' and we said we'd like a couple of armchairs and we had a red armchair and a green armchair. He was horrified when he saw them! How anybody could buy chairs of different colours. We went to the Ideal Home Exhibition in London and we saw a glass lamp with a Salvador Dali-like figure on it, hand painted, and we asked could we order one and it wasn't for sale. It had been specially produced for the exhibition and we said, 'When it's over, what happens?' and he didn't know and we gave him our name and address and weeks later we had a letter saying we could have the light, and we regret it got broken. I believe it would fetch thousands of pounds now because it really was a collector's piece.

Max Sinclair, born 1930

In my teenage years I felt very ashamed of my home ... which is a dreadful thing. When I went to Secondary Modern school, which was Harry Cheshire, it opened up a whole new world ... I was now mixing with a different kind of person. I lived up Hoo Road which has now been knocked down for the ring road but I met a girl who lived in Franche, and she wanted me to go up there ... I walked up there to her house. Well! It was a council house but it was the most beautiful thing I'd ever seen. There was a bathroom, hot water, a lavatory in the house! It was absolutely wonderful! You didn't go across a yard, all winds and weathers, to go to the lavatory – there was this room in the house. And amongst everything else, there was carpet on the floor. We didn't have carpet, there was a little bit of a rug ... it fascinated me really and I know I felt, at about eleven, that there was going to be more to my life than what I'd got, and I wanted there to be more. I don't mean I wanted big flash things because I never did, that wasn't me,

Astwood Farm is pictured in 1984, before its demolition.

but I certainly wanted more than what I'd got in Hoo Road.

Jean Nichols, born 1940

We moved then to George Street. It was more or less a rooming house because we weren't the only people there. We were on the third floor. My mother had thirteen of us – I'm the baby of the family ... and I'm the only one left out of thirteen. Somebody from the council came and they said, 'We got you a house, a council house up Tolladine'. Course, we didn't know what to expect, we kids. It was beautiful that house. It was a house, at last, on our own, our own grounds. It was a council house but to us it was a palace. At last we'd got something of our own, not to be shared with neighbours. You had your own door key and you could lock yourself in or lock yourself out. We thought we was in heaven ... whether it was that house we moved into, I don't know, but we seemed to have some luck. We got a bit more money coming in. That house proved to be very lucky.

Cath Wild, born 1929

Kath Robinson had been living with her parents-in-law and more recently with her parents while her husband put the finishing touches to their new home:

Our daughter was born in 1953 and she was five months old when we eventually moved into the bungalow. It was really very advanced. We had a lovely bathroom, we had central heating, which was hardly

29

heard of – my husband had done that as an experiment and it actually worked. We moved in on Hallowe'en. We'd got very little furniture, no carpets. The whole house echoed if anyone slammed a door! The bathroom was special because we'd actually got a coloured bathroom suite, which was quite something at that time. I was at work one day and my husband rang up and said, 'What coloured bathroom suite do you want?' I said, 'Pink!' and he said, 'Oh, that's a shame because it's green!' I've still got it today. I think the bungalow cost us about £1,200 to build. The kitchen was very basic. I had an electric cooker that cost about £2. It was very basic and my husband had taken it apart and cleaned every bit of it and put it together again. It was the best cooker I ever had.

Kath Robinson, born 1929

Jean Nichols has found her perfect home:

We've been here six years and we had this built. This was some ground that my father-in-law [had] … and this is my Shangri-La. Nothing could replace this. It's very special. I'm nearly two acres away from the nearest neighbour and I'd lived on a yard so this, to me, is just wonderful. I'd never want to move. My mum didn't live to see this built. She knew we were going to come here and [she] would have been as proud as punch to see us here but I know what [she] would have said to me, 'Ah Jeannie, don't you ever forget where you came from'. And I never will. I'm telling you this story now. I will never forget those roots … I feel now – look what I've got … there's magic in it and I don't want to be anywhere else.

Jean Nichols, born 1940

CHAPTER 3

Who are we?

Mary Macdiarmid (in foreground) at home with her family in Trinidad, Christmas 1959.

Stories of class distinction and beyond the green baize door. Where you fit in – and where you don't. From the travelling people and the gypsies to racial discrimination, the people of Worcestershire talk about who they are:

Ellis Wilson became part of the 'upstairs downstairs' world:

You felt proud of having a job in Croome Court. It was a lift up, different than farming or anything else. You felt you'd got a status in life. When I first walked in through the big door to meet the butler I looked around me and I was astounded at the size of the place. It was rather frightening for a bit. All the staff and everything was underground, it was all passages and I thought, 'My word, this is a big do!' Counting the outside, there were forty-one staff that I remember – there were twenty-one inside but then you'd got the gas men, the chauffeurs, the stable men. Then you'd got the gardeners, you see – there were six in the walled kitchen garden, which is the biggest walled kitchen garden in the country, so they say. The old lord – he just used to nod to you. You didn't see much of him upstairs. You kept away you see. You respected their isolation. They didn't want you to poke around. In any case you weren't allowed to go in and out of the rooms. You had to get permission to go. You never contacted them in any way. You didn't speak to them unless they spoke to you.

Ellis Wilson, born 1907

There was a distinct division between the classes. There were the wealthy and the non-wealthy. Wealthy people lived along the Hallow Road. I think there were four big houses – I mean a house where they kept a butler and a cook – and they were very nice people. They were benevolent. That is to say they were always kind and helpful when called upon to do so for the less able and less wealthy in the village. The last of the big houses belonged to Mrs Lea of Lea and Perrins Sauce. Mr Lea had built Hallow Church at the southern end of the village, standing by itself. There was some squabble in those days about finishing the church. Mr Lea, who was paying for most of it, wanted a tower. The vicar, the Reverend Pepys, wanted a spire and they couldn't agree. So they kept it like that [unfinished] until the old boy died, then Mrs Lea said, 'You can have your spire'. She was a very kind woman, a little autocratic. She almost had a village of her own – a laundry and this, that and the other. She sent all the poor villages a gift every Christmas, blankets, coal ... the trouble was the people who had the coal wanted the blankets and the people who had the blankets wanted the coal. There was always something wrong. I could never understand why they didn't appreciate her kindness and leave it at that. It was smacking a bit of the mediaeval times when the rich looked after the poor, but it was meant well.

Richard Clay, born 1905

H.M.S.ARK ROYAL

Chris Cookson joins the Royal Navy.

Chris Cookson found his niche in the Royal Navy:

Once I'd learnt to wear the uniform – you had to learn to fold everything right, and iron it right, and starch it right, or off it would come – ripped off you bodily sometimes if it was really bad. You had a set of trousers and I had five parallel creases on my trousers, at the bottom. It was done by height. If you were a tall guy you had seven. The idea behind it was in the old days they hadn't got much room, they could fold the trousers up and still look smart. So, you didn't have a vertical crease – you had parallel creases. Then a jacket, but underneath a white short-sleeved [shirt]. They call it a white front, a square-cut shirt. Then you had a blue collar, and that

had to be ironed properly. It was quite an operation to put one of these on!

Chris Cookson, born 1957

The great divide was in school times. We went to a primary school and at eleven years old there were the people who could afford to go to the secondary school and be paid for [who] departed from our school, and we felt we were left like the dregs in the bottom of the barrel. We were always at loggerheads, our school, with these toffee-nosed people at the tech. It gave us a feeling of insecurity … that we were deprived, and these other great fellows that had gone – the people we liked most in the school had all departed for this higher education that we were never going to get. They virtually went off into another life. We didn't see really that there was anything for us. The only thing we knew [was that] we were going to be working lads and work in a factory and the others were going to get good jobs. We were made to feel a little bit worthless, so we had to assert ourselves so we became a bit aggressive really, and I think all of the working lads of my age were a little bit aggressive for that reason.

Bert Batty, born 1908

Mary Macdiarmid was three years old when this photograph was taken in Trinidad.

There were always misunderstandings about gypsies and the travellers:

Some people would say, 'Gypsy, gypsy, live in a tent'. I'd take no notice. Whether you live in a tent, you're only flesh and blood like them. When I went to school for a few weeks and mum would give me an orange I'd say, 'Cut it four ways, mum. There's four of us play together'. And [other children would say] 'Look at her eating orange off a gypsy! I wouldn't eat off a gypsy! You don't know where their hands have been'. And I said, 'When I go to the loo I wash my hands as well as you wash your'n, and I wipe them on the towel'. 'Oh, I didn't think that.' They thought because you lived in a horse-drawn wagon, you hadn't got this and you hadn't got that. It's like a good many – they'll see my bit of washing out and if I tell them I do it by hand they'm shocked. I'm an old-fashioned traveller and I'll remain this way.

Harriet Hall, born 1922

Dad was in the amusement business. He used to think he was a travelling showman and I suppose to some extent he was. He had acquired a set of swing boats which he used to open in the valley all summer. Before the summer started (if the weather was suitable) he used to travel to the surrounding villages, like Highley and Stottesdon, with a set of swing boats, a kiddies' roundabout (hand turned – no power in those days!) a shooting gallery which was a Winchester 22, a coconut sheet and a football kicker. He used to travel round the villages and do perhaps three or four venues before

Easter then pull back into Habberley Valley for Easter. That's where we'd stay all summer and hopefully get a living by running these swing boats and things all summer.

Ron Jennings, born 1927

But gypsies weren't the only people who felt the stigma:

I think I was the first black person living in Studley at the time and it was bit of a problem. The children … used to wait for me outside their school gate. As soon as I approached they would start chanting, 'Blackie, Blackie!' and my mother-in-law used to get so upset and chase them off with a broom. But I used to say to her, 'Mum, they're only children and they're only repeating what their parents have said'. She would be really up in the air and say, 'I'm not having this!' This went on for a solid couple of weeks and I thought … 'I've got to find a way for these children' because it was a bit annoying, and all of a sudden I thought, 'Yes! I've got the solution to this'. There they were, outside waiting for me because they knew I came home for dinner and as soon as I approached they started chanting 'Blackie' and I shouted back, 'Whitie, Whitie, Whitie!' and they burst out laughing. The next day when they saw me coming up the road they all came to meet me and they were saying, 'You want a sweet?' And I became friends with them.

Madge Tilsley, born 1931

I used to phone for flats when I wanted to move. I never got to look at flats. People would think from the sound of my voice that I was a coloured person and I would be told flats had gone – or whatever. If I went round in person it was different. I found it and I still find it sad when I come across prejudice now. When I think back to growing up in the West Indies, a lot of people that left were people [who] saw coming to England as a new way of life – a chance to make something of themselves. And their families would fight and work so hard to save the money to send them to this country. Some were coming from very, very primitive ways of living. Houses that had no water out in the bush, that had no cooking facilities, and everybody lived in one room. They didn't know the culture here – the way of life – so they would come over as being ignorant and stupid but they weren't. I try very hard to fight against people being prejudiced because of the way a person looks – their colour.

Mary Macdiarmid, born 1948

I've never really come across individual racism. People have treated me how they've found me. I know it's there and I know it exists. I remember once, working at Quality Springs, one of the work mates, we were talking, reading the paper and somebody made a comment about foreigners and one of the girls said, 'Oh we don't mean you Madge. You're one of us!' I thought that was funny. I think it's how people find you.

Madge Tilsley, born 1931

Yvonne Welsh is seen with her family in India, 1960.

That's the thing that I liked the most. I was able to walk out at night with my two girls and there was no fear at all, and I liked it so much when I saw a boy holding a girl's hand. There was freedom which we didn't have. We did have it before independence. I think I'll always think of myself as Anglo-Indian – I can never say I'm English. There are differences but I'm quite happy here. What I miss is now we're getting older we definitely feel it would be nice to see people around. You never felt alone in India because there were people all around you and there were people in worse circumstances than you. So you never felt that you were suffering or not getting enough because there was always somebody worse than you. Here, we feel a bit more isolated.

Yvonne Welsh, born 1929

Yvonne Welsh in England, 1960.

To finish – a story of dual nationality:

We went to Southsea, a day trip on a coach outing, and I went into a newsagent's to get a newspaper. 'Ah' he said, 'I know where you're from'. I thought he was going to say the West Indies, but he said, 'The Midlands!' I thought, 'Oh Madge, you've arrived at last!' He said, 'You've got a Midlands accent'. I'm Redditch through and through but I must tell you, to come back [to the West Indies] it was like I was going home. It was such a strange thing. On the way going I sat next to a chap, a white chap. I took it that he was going on holiday so I got talking to him and said, 'You going on holiday?' and he said, 'No, I'm going home to Jamaica'.

And I thought, 'Gosh, that's great!' There are some things that will always be Jamaican but there's some things I love about England. So really I've got dual nationality.

Madge Tilsley, born 1931

CHAPTER 4

Money and the workplace

The Wilkes family is pictured in 1917. The children in the back row are, from left to right: Winnie (age ten), Frank (age thirteen), and May (age twelve). Elsie (age five) is between her parents at the front.

Frank and May Wilkes in 1906.

From colourfinding in the carpet industry to donning a blue serge uniform. From Royal Worcester Porcelain to the Coronation gloves – the people of Worcester look back on their place of work, and reflect on what it was like to have a job for life:

Frank Wilkes was awarded an MBE for long service to the County Council:

This is my MBE and it's a silver medal with a crown on the top and the King and Queen in the centre of the medallion. It's a very valuable medal as far as I'm concerned. I started work in March 1918 and I was thirteen and a half. I was the junior clerk and

the 'dogsbody' around the office and I had to be running the messages between offices. There was only one telephone in the County Surveyor's room. If people wanted to speak between the offices in the same building we had to do it by speaking tubes – tubes about one inch, one and a half-inch diameter down the walls, and at each end of the tube there was a mouthpiece and a little whistle which fitted in the mouthpiece. If you wanted to speak to another room you pulled the whistle out, put the mouthpiece to your mouth and blew hard and that would sound the whistle at the other end of the tube. We used to like to play jokes – we'd often get a few dried peas and put them down the speaking tube, or a drop of water! It

Ted Taylor at Worcester Porcelain, 1982.

Ted Taylor at Worcester Porcelain, 1998.

was all meant in good fun!

Frank Wilkes, born 1904

Artistic talent led Ted Taylor into a career at Worcester Porcelain:

I left school early. I didn't take school certificate or GCSE, whatever they call it these days. I left at sixteen – I wanted to start work. I wanted to paint and my eldest sister, being in charge of the family, she suggested I put my school paintings together and try and get a job at Royal Worcester, which I did and they offered me this job which I'd never heard of before – copperplate engraver. I thought it was very interesting. The initial part of the apprenticeship was very trying. I couldn't believe you could work all day and achieve nothing because we were working on a very small area of copperplate with one single tool. I wanted to get onto something with a bit of form to it, like leaves or motifs of some sort. I quickly made friends with one elderly gentleman, who I sat by. I fetched and carried for him and he looked after me. He put me right on tool sharpening, which is very, very important in this trade. Some of the earliest jobs I did were small contract jobs for personalised dinnerware with monograms on which were overlaid letters. I felt good going in there. Good, but nervous. There was a pervading smell in the department. This was because everyone innocently smoked in those days, so the foreman smoked a pipe, one of the senior engravers smoked a pipe, two others smoked Player's cigarettes, very strong, but the whole department was wreathed in tobacco smell and old clothes. I always imagined I could smell old clothes. The older men in the department would wear a shirt all the week and just change the collar, because they were detachable collars and they would have a collar stud front and back. And when they got to work they would take their top coats off and remove the detachable collar and put it under a piece of paper so that it got no contamination on it and they'd put it on and look lovely and crisp to go home … if you could make a detachable collar last two days it was good going. When I went there, there were thirteen engravers – at that time, the inklings of modern transfer printing technology were being formed by specialist printing companies, mainly in Stoke on Trent pottery area. So, as people retired from Royal Worcester in the engraving department, they weren't replaced because these modern methods had come in – it reduced the ranks somewhat, and I wouldn't mind saying in the whole of the industry in this country there's certainly no more than thirty still working. There are two where I work, and in eighteen months' time we both retire and we won't be replaced. I think some of the quality of the fine work will be difficult to achieve using other means. I don't wish to knock modern technology. The cutting of a steel tool into metal is so fine and precise, if a line of that quality is attempted using any other medium you will not match the engraved line.

Ted Taylor, born 1935

The Moorings, in Pershore.

Colourfinding, carpet pickers and a whole new community:

My father was working as a weaver at Morris Carpets. He got me a job so I started at fifteen in the carpet industry. I was what they called a 'colourfinder'. The loom would make a mistake and a carpet picker, always ladies in those days, would sew in the mistake by hand. So, this job I went to do, colour finding, lasted for six months. You would go and find the colour, the yarns that the ladies needed to repair. It was a super thing to be part of this community at work with all these girls. The older ladies would be talking about people. Someone that had died, got married, divorced, had an affair, all sorts of things like this, and this little fifteen-year-old that I was, was there, listening avidly, wishing so much that I knew who they were talking about. People helped each other. I knew fifteen, sixteen, seventeen-year-olds had boyfriends, and if you fell out with your boyfriend there was always someone ready to [say] 'You come to the Labour Club with us, you'll be alright'. If we were going to go to the dance at Birmingham, instead of twos and threes travelling in a car, you didn't have a car then, you went on a coach – a great feeling of camaraderie.

Kath Barnett, born 1942

Tom Mayo spent much of his working life on the boats. He started when he was a youngster:

Boating was never an easy life but it wasn't too hard for a youngster because I didn't have to carry the cargoes, but my dad did. I used to follow behind the horse and work the locks for my dad, and so did my sisters and my other brothers. Being a lad, when I got to about twelve, I got capable of handling anything – I was big enough to work the locks on my own. Then my dad had an easy life. When I was fifteen, I was carrying sacks of sugar and sacks of wheat and loading the boat then.

Tom Mayo, born 1916

Things have changed enormously. When I started at Brockways in '66 the weaver would have his loom. If his loom was number twelve then he would tend that loom always. We closed our weaving department down three years ago and decided to concentrate totally on tufting, but in the end of this, the man would not go every day to number twelve and work his eight-hour shift there. He would have to be far more flexible. He would go wherever he was sent; and this word 'flexible,' in industry, is what we've all become. I've not forgotten my roots. I've not forgotten that I had the lowliest job at the factory when I started at Brockway Carpets – the simplest job to do. In about 1977, '78, I remember a warehouse manager we had then saying to me, 'I bet you'll finish up on the Board one day'. No way! And it was a surprise to me when I was invited to be a director, still, four or five years ago. I suppose because of my roots as this Kidderminster child that had lived in a two-up, two-down, [it was] never ever thought that she would be a director on the board of a successful company.

Kath Barnett, born 1942

I went down to Brockway Carpets and asked if they'd got any jobs and they said yes. I had no qualifications and Kidderminster was carpets and there were that many factories you could take your pick. I was very nervous, I think I was still wearing my school shirts. I was a bobbin boy. That's when the winders get the hanks of yarn, wind them onto bobbins and then they are put into a truck and then the bobbin boy collects the bobbins and pushes the trucks to the looms and stacks the yarn at the looms ready for them to be wove. I did that for twelve months and you get to learn the colours and the names of the colours and the numbers. After that, I went into the picking room. I wanted to be a weaver. It was six years continuous service [as an apprentice].

John Smith, born 1952

Gill and Robin opened their own restaurant. They relive their first day:

We took over the restaurant five or six years ago. A restaurant in a garden centre came up for rent so we thought we'd give it a bash. We didn't have to lay out a lot of money because it was on a weekly rental basis. We call it a coffee shop but it's really a restaurant. The first morning we opened, it was quite scary, quite tense. We put the signs out on the road and waited for people to come in. I think we did about six meals and took £20. It took about two and a half years to get established. We did have dead days in the beginning. People are much more happy to go out for a meal now. It

John Smith is seen with his broadloom at Brockway Carpets.

doesn't have to be an occasion.

Robin MacAllistair, born 1957

Bert Batty charts his career:

The 1930s was the Great Depression. I was out of work and I joined the dole queue and that was the most degrading experience of my life because when I got there I saw the best tradesmen in the building trade in this queue to go and get their 12 shillings a week, or 15 shillings a week or whatever it was. It was virtually thrown at us. I got in this queue and I thought, 'It can't be just me – all these wonderful tradesmen are joining this queue'. It was really degrading. And then, the Depression was starting to go and it was the era of the 'spec' builders,

building houses all over the place – building houses, and houses fast. This was brought about by the solicitors realising this was a great opportunity for them to get hold of conveyancing fees and so on, so they would finance people like me who wanted to start up. I had seen in Redditch some boards up for some land for sale in Studley Road, and I looked at this from time to time because I was doing a bit of courting down that way and I thought, like so many of us at that time, 'Where are we going to get the money from to get married?' and I had a look at this 'for sale' board and I thought, 'Why shouldn't I be part of this scheme?' And I went and saw this solicitor – great day – he decided that he would finance me and we would go on from there. I bought this land through him for six houses. Now then, they say,

'Fools step in where angels fear to tread' and this is exactly what I did. I could have a draw of money when the first foundations were in, and it was getting over that first week. To borrow money in those days was something almost impossible. Banks wouldn't look at you if you hadn't got a rich family behind you. I went on and went on, worrying all the week as to where the money was going to come from to pay the wages. In the end I managed to get the first pair of foundations in, so I got my draw and on we went! So, eventually I completed the houses, got them sold – it was absolutely wonderful! It was a great thing I had done. From having nothing and no money in my pocket and no future I suddenly had a future and I could think about getting married, which I did.

Bert Batty, born 1908

Tina Dodd describes her start in the Police Force:

It was actually dad's idea for me to join the Police Force, and there was an advert in the *Evening News* for police cadets, which meant you could go at sixteen, or sixteen and a half, into the cadets scheme – so that's what I did. I went for the entrance exam and got in. My recollection of training is only good. You're part of a team and you're working together. Okay, you're a girl, and respect was there for that fact. I mean, lifesaving was a hoot. You used

Bert Batty, his mother, and brother Tom are shown here in the 1900s.

Bert marries Zona in 1934.

to have to do lifesaving. I'm not flat-chested by any means, and they used to draw lots to see who could rescue me from the swimming pool! In the end I got teamed up with this lad called Sean, who isn't in this job anymore, and he was built like a stick bean – he was so thin! He was equally embarrassed as I was to be partnered up, but it was all taken in the good spirit that it was meant and there was no offence meant at all. When you're in situations when you've got to work hard and play hard together there was a camaraderie that develops and you don't forget those people that you made friends with all those years ago. It is like a big family. I think it makes you more confident as a person. When I talk to people they will

never believe that I haven't always been assertive and confident. Personally, I've grown and developed. That is all through the work environment and the support you get and also the situations that you find yourself in. At the end of the day when you are wearing a blue serge uniform, and you're representing the Police Force, the public expect you to deal with those situations – even if underneath your knees are knocking, you've got to do that job

Tina Dodd, born 1957

And finally, the making of the Coronation gloves for the future Queen of England:

When I left school, which you had to do at fourteen, there wasn't a lot of work about. I just went round from factory to factory to see if they wanted anyone. Eventually, my uncle worked at Fownes in the office and they wanted an apprentice in the fur department. They sent me an exam which I passed and they offered me the job – apprenticed for four years. It was considered a safe job. Fownes was a top factory, a good firm to work for – the first firm to do paid holidays for the workers. It had a smashing clubhouse near the factory, billiards and canteen and everything. In those days there were some fairly large rooms. The glove cutters, there were two or three different rooms of glove cutters and there was machinists, about 400 of those in one large long room along the front of the building. The room I was in, the fur-cutting room – there was about twelve working in there. We was on the side overlooking the canal at the back and you could see the boss in his office, Dickie Bird his name was! Another firm in Worcester – their manager was named Charlie Sparrow and he used to come to Fownes occasionally and we'd look down, 'Oh they'm together again – Bird and Sparrow'. We used to have a laugh about that. In the 1930s when the slump set in, we started getting a lot of foreign imports into the glove trade – cheap stuff from Italy … so we went onto short time, about three days a week and then it got worse. The married men went onto two days a week but the single ones – we only had one day a week. We used to meet and go for long walks in the country. Four of us had to put together to get enough for a packet of Woodbines – tuppence. So, you can tell how serious it was, then. One day, looking in the paper again, 'Wanted: coloured leather sorter'. I hadn't done any leather sorting but I know the trade, got the job at Dent Allcroft. I was to be assistant to the main sorters. After a time, the Coronation cropped up and Dents got the job. We went through about 100 of the best leathers they got, the best skins, picked out the ten best and then we handed it on to the cutter. It was all covered in gold, and eventually I saw the Queen wearing them at the Coronation. You can't get any higher than that in the trade than doing the Coronation gloves!

Jim Beechey, born 1908

CHAPTER 5
Living together

Lilly Peach's wedding, 1948.

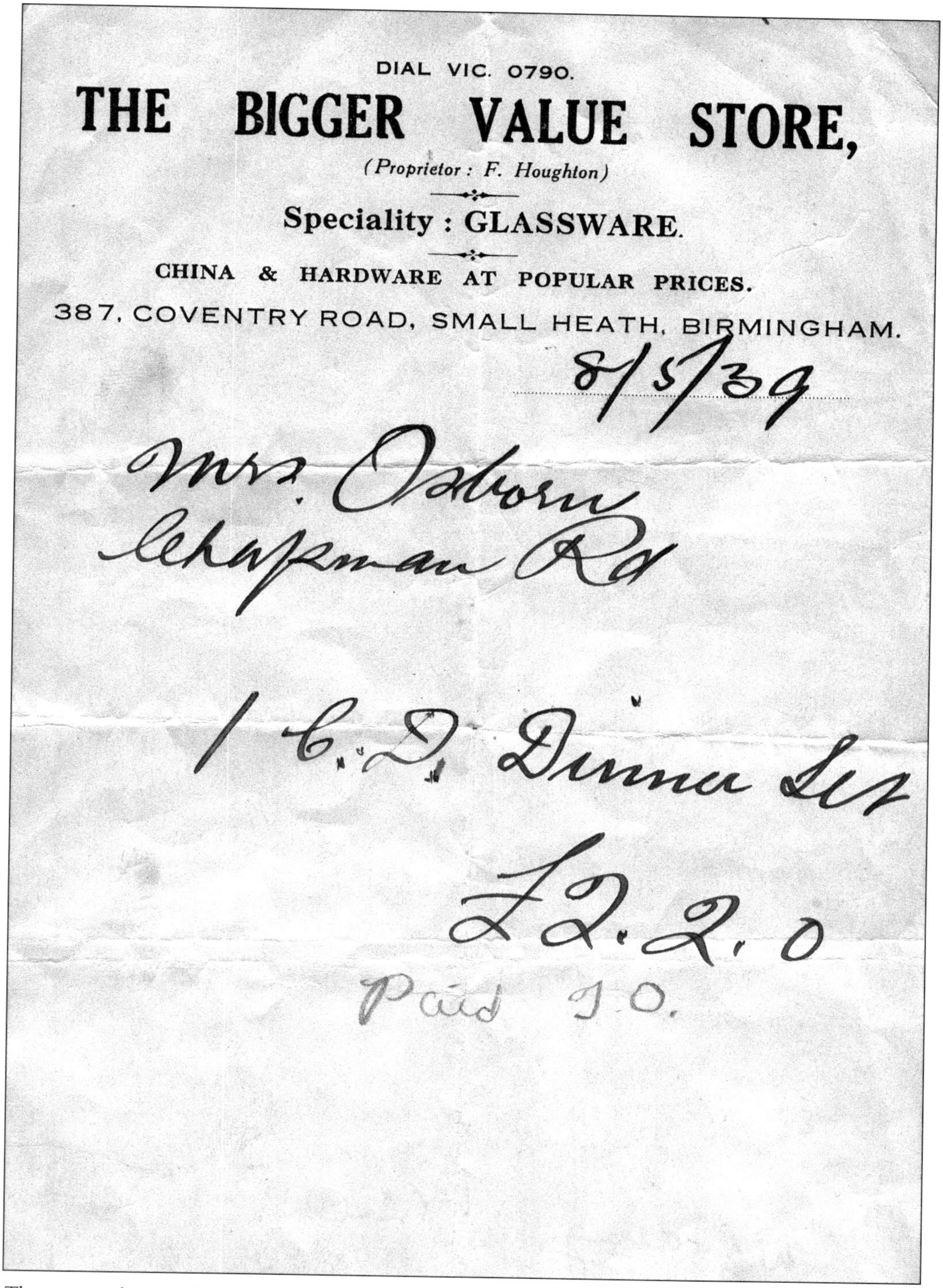

THE BIGGER VALUE STORE,

(Proprietor : F. Houghton)

Speciality : GLASSWARE.

CHINA & HARDWARE AT POPULAR PRICES.

387, COVENTRY ROAD, SMALL HEATH, BIRMINGHAM.

8/5/39

Mrs. Osborn
Chapman Rd

1 C.D. Dinner Set

£2. 2. 0

Paid J.O.

This receipt for a wedding gift dates from 1939.

From the can can girl at the Commando base, and an office romance, to finding out where babies come from at the last minute! The people of Worcestershire talk candidly about their experiences of love, sex, and marriage:

Cath Wild reveals an intimate moment:

At that age I didn't know where babies come from. I know it's hard to believe but we wasn't given any sex instruction, and what bit of sex we did pick up, it was learnt on the fair, in the clubs, and you just picked that up from your mates. Whether it was true or not you didn't know. But aged eighteen I did not know where babies come from! They'd say if we kissed a chap we'd have a baby! I mean, it is silly. We laughed at it now. Anyway, the first time we done it was about two and a half years [after we'd been going out together] … he said, 'How much longer have I got to wait?' It was up against the hedge. He was fumbling and I was fumbling. We'd never done it before, you see. Never had sex in my life before, till then, and me saying 'Oh hurry up, hurry up – I've got to get home!' And then I just run from him. Well, we've laughed after that – I just left him and I run home. But, that was my first experience, by the hedge. I couldn't look at him the next time he come to my house!

Cath Wild, born 1929

My stepdad said, 'You've got to have somebody to go round with'. I didn't like the idea. This chap took me to the pictures. It was a shilling to go in.

'We'll have something to eat,' he said, 'when we go out.' He walked into this chip shop, buys these chips – but he never bought two papers full – he bought one! A shilling for the chips. He got on this bench and he said, 'Come on, tuck in!' and I said, 'Stuff you and your chips! I'm going home to where I can fill my belly'. I said to dad, 'No [not] him dad! He'd skin a gnat's eye for a ha'penny!'

Harriet Hall, born 1922

Office romances were discouraged where Lynne worked:

I remember the second day, walking into the office, and this guy was just about to press the lift button to close the door and go to his office, and he saw me coming and he said, 'What floor do you want?' and I said, 'Three, please' and his first words were, 'Are you new?' and I said, 'Yes'. 'What, permanent or temporary?' So that's how we met – we met in the lift. I did think, 'You're somebody I'd like to know better'. And he has an aura of 'don't get too close' about him and that always makes me feel quite safe, you see. His parents went away for a long weekend and he decided to throw a party. They have a terraced garden, and he was doing guided tours of the garden by torchlight and I was the only one (it was about two in the morning) who hadn't been on a guided tour. And I thought, 'How can I get this guy on his own?' So I said, 'I'd like a guided tour now, please'. So we went down the garden to see the pond and the frogs at the bottom of the garden and, just by accident, I tripped and he

50

caught me and kissed me! It wasn't allowed. It was actually in our contracts that you weren't to associate with other members of staff. Now, whether that was to discourage affairs I don't know but it was actually written in so we had to have an almost illicit love affair. We had to meet in the park after work where nobody could see us and we went on with this and it didn't occur to either of us how silly this was. We were both single people that were allowed to do this. It never occurred to us. We were so worried about our jobs we kept it a secret for a very long time! We got found out when we went to the theatre together and one of the Office Partners, I didn't know was involved with the Swan Theatre, was on the door that night and took our tickets.

Lynne Hunter, born 1959

Tony Baxter's reputation suffered because she used to show her garters on stage:

We were on the commando base. Our boys, the ratings from the camp, and one or two of the officers used to go out in their LCDs and storm a beach and make it safe for the army. I did the entertainments, which is how I met my husband. We were putting on a concert and I was in a group of can can girls and he was the lights operator. He was laid on a beam in the roof, shining the floodlights onto us as we flicked our skirts and showed our garters! He was extremely quiet – suffered a great inferiority complex – didn't think anybody would ever notice him. I think I took that as a challenge and sort of

said, 'I think I can alter that!' So, if things go wrong now I do sometimes in my mind blame myself. I think, 'Well, you engineered it!' Camp pitched in and did the whole thing for us. The WRNS Galley did all the cooking. They issued a day of holiday for the whole camp. The gunnery officer was my best man.

Tony Baxter, born 1909

It was nearly a shotgun wedding for Joyce:

I met my husband, in the Priory Lodge hall (dance hall) because if they didn't have [something] going on in the

Chris Cookson's wedding, 1981.

Tony Baxter's husband-to-be.

Tony Baxter's wedding at the commando base.

The wedding party at Tony Baxter's marriage.

Two-year-old Bert Batty poses in a suit knitted by his grandmother.

Winter Gardens it was at the Priory Lodge. When he came home on leave (he was going abroad) I went up to his mother's and then things started and I got pregnant. I had to tell my mother. Well, my mother used to check all our periods anyway. Of course she was very wild at the time, and my dad was, she wrote to his mother and told her and said we'd got to get married. They made arrangements for the wedding. Anyway, I had a miscarriage in the August so I wrote and told him we wouldn't have to get married now because I'm alright, but he still wanted to come back to England to get married so they moved him back and we got married in the October. There were four of us from the factory got married that year, and we all borrowed each other's wedding dresses and bridesmaids' dresses. I had five bridesmaids – my sister got married a couple of years after so she was using

Bert with his mother and a wickerwork perambulator, 1909.

some of the dresses, borrowing.

Joyce Tandy, born 1926

I had Carol on the Tuesday, but I started in labour on the Saturday and the nurse come and she said, 'You're not ready, you're not big enough to have a child' … anyway, she was born on the Tuesday afternoon – she was six-pounds-something. I always remember her saying to me [the nurse] 'Have you got a razor?' and I thought, 'What does she want a razor blade for?' She said, 'I must shave you'. And I said, 'In the bathroom. My husband's razor'. And I remember her shaving me and she put the razor in the windowsill, and when my husband came to use his razor he couldn't find it and I said, 'It's in the windowsill – Nurse Downe had it' and he said, 'What did she have it for?' And I told

him and he said, 'Well, she could have washed it!' He was most annoyed!

Joyce Tandy, born 1926

I was in the ward talking to this girl I knew and I said I didn't know where babies come from, and I was just stood at the bottom of her bed and I said, 'Oop, I can't move!' and she said, 'What's the matter?' and I said, 'I just can't move'. I'd got no pain. I just felt I couldn't move. So, she rang the bell and two nurses came and said, 'Come along Mrs Wild' and I said, 'I'm alright, I just can't move. Something's happening down here and I can't move'. It beggars belief that a married woman shouldn't know all about childbirth but as I said we were never taught about sex. Anyway, they told me after in the ward, they said, 'You aren't in there five minutes and then

The christening of Cynthia Pearson's son.

[we heard the baby cry]. First baby!' And I said, 'Goodness gracious me, if that's having a baby I don't mind having a dozen!'

Cath Wild, born 1929

Joyce's first marriage ended tragically while her children were still young:

Caroline was thirteen, Marilyn was ten, Cathy was nine, and Barbara was eight when he died. He came home on this Saturday with these pains and things and we phoned for the doctor to come and he came on the Monday morning and he said, 'I think he's got meningitis'. On the Friday morning he [the doctor] looked in again and he said, 'We'd better take him into hospital'. I couldn't go in at night because [I couldn't leave the children] then at eight o'clock on the Saturday morning the police come and I had to go into the hospital. He was in a coma and he died. He died at one o'clock. Father Firth came down and they took the children into my neighbours and he told them he'd gone to Jesus. He had to tell them. I couldn't tell them. For three months I was on Valium tablets. My mother-in-law lived over the road so she came over and stopped with me and I went on Social Security and the Social Security man came and said to me, 'Would you like to go back to work? We'll put your children in a home. You're only thirty-five, you could go back to work'. I said no – I wouldn't put my children in a home – no way. They wanted to do a post-mortem on Ray and I said, 'No, he didn't want to be cut about when he was alive, I'm not having him cut about

now'. I had Carol and Marilyn sleeping with me in the bed after Ray died and the mother went back home, and this one night, I suppose it was the first night I'd been on my own, and mother-in-law had gone back, and I'd got a glass at the table by the side of the bed and I'd got my Valium tablets and I thought, 'I've got to take these' and Marilyn (she was ten) said 'Mum, what would happen if you died? We haven't got a dad nor a mum'. And I said, 'I'm not going to die!' So of course that brought me out of things, then anyway the doctor come in the next day and I told him what had happened and he said, 'Give me the tablets' and it was a coal fire and he threw them all on the fire and said, 'I'm not giving you no more tablets!'

Joyce Tandy, born 1926

I've always been afraid of the dark ... which I still am, as old as I am. And I've always been afraid on my own but of course when he died I went away for a week, but I said to them, 'I've got to go back home'. They said, 'You can't go on your own' and I said, 'I've got nobody else to go with. I can't uproot the family. They've got their own families to look after'. So I came back, and the first night I think I just lay in bed but I wasn't sleeping – I was taut, strung up and frightened that [it was] the first time I'd slept there since he died. Lying on your own in a double bed. They say as time goes on it heals. I don't think it ever do, it don't ever heal Especially when he was the only man I ever had. The only man I ever courted. The only man I'd slept with.

Cath Wild, born 1929

To finish – a story of bravery and hope:

We won a trip, through one of the sweet companies, Trebor, to go to Borneo. It was a long way to go. It was going to be a wrench leaving the children but it was an experience too good to miss and it was something we very much wanted to do [and] it was free! We went on to Singapore and I remember phoning home one night and mum's voice was different and I didn't know why and I said, 'Is there something wrong?' And she said 'No, no, we're fine'. So we got home the following Sunday and mum took me into the kitchen, quietly, and said to me the warehouse was ram raided, thieves had taken a Range Rover, driven through the roller shutter doors and taken £30,000 worth of stock. There was loads of damage. It was just an awful thing and it had happened on that day. Three weeks later to that day exactly the same thing happened again and they found another way in. This time my husband was devastated, Paul was just devastated. It 'cracked him up' to coin a phrase. He just didn't know how to cope with it. He came in and the warehouse was wrecked and stuff had been taken. He began to fear the phone ringing and I had to tell people not to ring me after nine at night. It didn't matter who it was. Paul would get palpitations and sweats and have to have a drink because he was so worried about the phone ringing … things were about as bad as they could get. The crime had got to him. He had almost a complete breakdown. He felt suicidal. The doctors seemed not to be able to help him. He had counselling – that couldn't help him. He was taking anti-

depressants, and he just felt he was worthless. And it just got worse and worse until one Sunday morning when I was getting changed to go to church and I found a lump on my breast and I remember thinking, 'This has got to be as bad as it's going to get. This really can't be happening!' And I even knew, and I'm not a pessimist, I'm an optimist, 'This is cancer. I know it is,' because this is how my life is going now. It's just going to be like this.

I really wanted to be rid of the lump. Losing the breast was insignificant at that point because being rid of the lump became more important. In the gaps in between the hospital appointments, I kept feeling this lump and thinking, 'I wish it would go away. I started hating it and wanting to push it away'. I could see it – I could look down and see it – probably nobody else could but I could … and I just wanted it to not be there. The only way that could happen was to lose the breast, and I'd never been in hospital being ill before. I'd never had an anaesthetic before and I was very, very frightened and the night I went into hospital … I started to cry and be sick at about seven o'clock and I finished at two in the morning. That's the only time I really, really broke down and all the time Paul is still having a nervous breakdown! I didn't know they did this with all operations but they drew a huge arrow pointing to the lump on me and I remember thinking, 'That's really basic. What a basic thing to do. Drawing on me as if I'm a piece of meat, really'. And I then had to face waking up. I was terribly poorly after the anaesthetic, and I'm also allergic to certain sickness drugs so it was a day or two before I could actually adjust to the fact that I only had one breast and I was swollen and bruised as well. And then on Sunday morning they said, 'Do you want to go to church?' And I did want to. The chapel was next door and I said, 'Yes, I do, very much want to go'. And they said, 'Would you like a shower first?' and I said, 'Yes, but I don't think I can look'. So they took me in and nurse stayed with me the whole time and she took the dressing off and she said, 'What do you want to do?' and I said, 'Well, I've got to look, haven't I?' And I did, and I felt dizzy and faint for a moment and I thought, 'It's gone'. And all I could think about was 'So's the lump'. Then I went off and took communion and I felt a bit better.

We were very nervous. Bearing in mind, it was only the all clear for a certain area of my body – but it was still the all clear for the next three months and the first thing he said was the scan was fine. Then he went on talking about other things and I realised that everybody was in the waiting room and I had to send Paul out to tell them it was okay – and for them that four minutes that I'd delayed it was like a lifetime to them! Then we got home, we drank champagne, went out for dinner and we did party a little bit. All the way through, I've mentioned the dramas of life and how you go through life with these little dramas until you come to a trauma – and you realise that those dramas have been there for you to face up to a huge problem – and I think it's

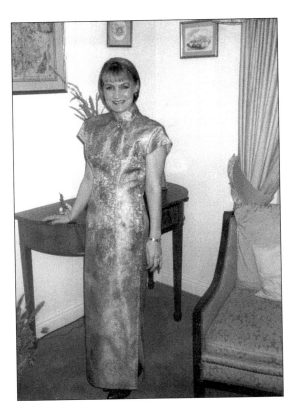

Lynne Hunter, in February 1998, dressed up for a formal evening. She was a third of the way through her chemotherapy treatment at the time.

Lynne Hunter, enjoying a few precious days in France with her family, in April 1998.

there in all of us. Somewhere you get an inner strength, and all those dramas that we think are so big when they happen to us – when something big really does happen you are prepared and you do come through it. I don't even know how exactly. It's just it did and I have. The one thing I grieve for now that I am well is my breast. I still have a bit of a problem not having a breast now. I said before about how lovemaking was something we grew together and became special. As we got older it got better. We had to start that all over again because I didn't know how he was going to feel about me, plus it hadn't been a significant part in our lives anyway because he'd been so ill. So the first time that happened was quite important and I can remember it was just a very special moment and it was just gentle and

wonderful. That was a very special morning for me and I will always remember it. I'll remember the date anyway because it was the first time, and I realised Paul still loved me as a woman as much as for myself – and that was quite special.

Lynne Hunter, born 1959

CHAPTER 6
Crime and the law

The police station and police houses in Pershore were built in the 1930s and closed in 1999.

Has crime increased over the century? Or is it that we know so much more about it now. Starting earlier this century, poaching, burglary and scrumping come under discussion and, as the years roll on, what it's like to be a police woman with a six inch truncheon! Worcestershire examines the crime figures:

I found somebody trying to break in at the lodge. I could see from the big house. It was winter and there were no leaves on the trees. [There was] something moving round by the lodge so I went to investigate and there was a very large man trying to break in and, of course, he heard me and he came towards me with a penknife in his hand and I thought, 'Any minute now I'm going to be stabbed!' but he got quite close then turned and ran. I ran back home and phoned the police. I had to go to court of course and the Inspector came to me afterward and said, 'A moment Mrs Beard, you didn't really do that very well' and I said, 'I'm sorry?' He said, 'Next time would you mind letting them break in? We can keep them for longer, that way'.

Margot Beard, born 1912

We did a lot of poaching! Billy Bullock's ground went along our ground (that we shot on) and father said, 'There's rabbits in that berry, there'. And I said, 'We can't do that, half of it's on Billy Bullock's ground'. He said, 'Slip over, he ain't about, and we'll put some nets on and put the ferrets in'. So we did, and lo and behold, here's Billy Bullock coming over the field. He [dad] said, 'Quick, go and get the nets!' But the ferret wouldn't come out. So, we ran down into the woods and blast me if the ferret didn't come out as he [Billy] got to the bush and he picked him up! ... [Dad met with another man who worked with Billy Bullock] and he said, 'Billy's got our ferret' and the man said, 'Oh, it's yours is it? You'll have to be quick because Wednesday he's taking him to market to sell him'. So father said to me, 'C'mon, we're going out tonight'. I said, 'Where we going?' and he said, 'We're going to Billy's. He's got out ferret in a little cage in the barn'. So I said, 'How are we going to find him?' and he said, 'I'll show you how to find him'. So we went down, no lights, and my dad [called the ferret] and the next thing you heard was the ferret scratching on the front of the box and we had our ferret back!

Francis Bird, born 1926

Policewoman Tina Dodd believes she has the best job in the world:

If you talk to the general public, if you say, 'What would you like out of the Police Force?' they will say a bobby on the beat [but] we haven't got the resources to do it. In Worcester we've got two local beat officers – one that works on Dines Green and one that works the Arboretum and the Wylds Lane area, and those are the only two local dedicated beat officers in the city. We've got the people who we call the responsive police. If you call in, they react, they go and deal with it, then they'll go on to the next one, and

Chris Cookson was on the mountain bike patrol. This photograph of him, with a colleague, was taken in 1997.

if you had a problem again tomorrow, it wouldn't necessarily be the same person that came to that problem because it could be a different shift, or a different member on that shift. I'm sure there are occasions when they would love to take just that little bit extra time but because the radio is going saying, 'Come on, you've got to go to the next job!' they are under pressure to go to the next one. But it's down to money isn't it? Money, and directives from the Home Office and I'm sure that here, Worcester, is no different from the rest of the country and any other Police Forces – that we are busy, and yes, I think it would be lovely to have more community-orientated police officers. This is the way that ACPO and the Home Office

want to see things going, and from my point of view it's a gift of a job because it's working with people and it's helping with people and I think, 'Blimey, I'm getting paid for it as well'. It's just brilliant!

Tina Dodd, born 1957

I remember joining up, that was in September '74 because that was the first time I was away from home. That was big change time, the '70s, because that's when the Equal Opportunities laws came in. Up until then, policewomen had a policewomen's department so they worked separately to the blokes. They only dealt with females and juveniles so you weren't on the same pay, you were on less pay.

Then the equality laws came in and they said, 'Right, we're going to disband the policewomen's department. You'll work shifts, you'll do the same job as the blokes and you'll be on the same pay'. So it was quite a big change. It was quite interesting because they were very protective to us as women and I was the only girl on my shift anyway and you would never, as a female, get sent to a job on your own, then. Now, it's totally different because you're just a piece of the manpower.

Tina Dodd, born 1957

My father was a policeman. He served at Worcester, then the Lye, then Stourbridge, Malvern, Pershore and finally back to Great Malvern. In 1931 he was involved in the first motor patrol. It started off with motorbikes and sidecars and progressed to motor cars and he was one of about six people who was present when it was formed. They concentrated on traffic matters and had to become expert on traffic law. They travelled all the roads in the county but in later years they broke it up into two divisions: one to cover the north of the county and one, the south. They didn't have radios then and initially they found problems were caused by absence of communication. The only way they could stop a car was to send a policeman out into the street in the hope that there was one coming by, and he would signal it to stop. They then devised a fairly Heath Robinson method of trying to communicate, of fixing a length of wood with an arrow at one end to the

Chris Cookson, on duty at Stourport Carnival.

John Hemming in 1999.

all those sorts of things. You carried handcuffs and if necessary you would have arrested people and put handcuffs on them. Policemen have always carried truncheons, the standard Dixon of Dock Green truncheons, and in the '70s, policewomen going out must have a truncheon as well. Their dilemma was where are we going to keep this truncheon, because policemen have a pocket which is hidden down the outside of their trouser leg so they wear the truncheon in there. So they actually issued us with a truncheon that was no more than about six inches long for the simple reason we could carry it in our handbags! Now, this is serious! You're walking down the high street and you're about to arrest somebody and you've got to furtle in your handbag and in the bottom of it you find this little, six-inches-long piece of wood and when you produce it and say, 'I'm arresting you!' everybody falls about laughing because they think it's a wind up! So, I never used my truncheon, I left it in my locker. That was the change – when you think about it now, the Police Force has gone through tremendous change in twenty years, that now policemen and policewomen go on self defence courses together. We now have the extendable baton we all wear on the utility belt and the training is equal and the officers use the equipment on an equal footing.

Tina Dodd, born 1957

I was scared of Worcester police. They were total bullies. Whether they had a hang-up (they hadn't gone away in the wars to fight) they were creeping

notice boards that were outside every police station. They fixed it with a screw that wasn't over-tightened so the arrow could be rotated, and if a car was known to be in the area they would phone the police station and say, 'Can you put the arrow at vertical?' The police cars looked out for this vertical arrow if they passed, and if they spotted it they would stop and use the telephone at the station to ring headquarters for further instructions.

John Hemming, born 1931

You relied on your mouth. You relied on the techniques you'd been taught of talking a situation down, calming people, body language, around some police station, dodging, exempt. In them days you could be laying in bed and the police just walked in, got you out of bed, questioned you. There was no: 'You'd got to have an adult there while you were being questioned' and all that. Turn the house over, 'This is stolen property – where did you get this?' 'Well, it ain't mine'. I suppose I was nine and I knew all the people who were thieving, and I suppose five of us had the birch. I broke into a house on Rainbow Hill and stole a few things and all that, and my pal, he got caught with a ring and we were ordered to have six strokes of the birch. This fellow, he came out of the room first and I heard this thing fly through the air, 'thwack', and he come out, and he wasn't crying none and I looked down and he was just pulling his trousers up and I see all the blood running. Then they grabbed me – two on each leg and one on each arm and they banged you on the cushion and proceeded to give it to you. It took about eight of them to hold me, a little kid, squirming about. You were left then to your own devices. The doctor he put iodine on the millions and millions of scratches. Walked up to the bus stop on the Cross with our mum, and I got on the bus and I couldn't sit down on the bus and our mum said, 'Oh he's just had the birch' – you know the way they go on. Women.

Anonymous

In small communities, because you were a policeman's son you were held in a little bit of apprehension because you might go telling tales to your father. So it wasn't too easy, in a new community, in a small community, to make friends. You were subjected to bullying at school – perhaps someone whose father may have run foul of the police, perhaps his son thought that was a way of making the scores equal. I don't know. I was, on occasions bullied, but one had to learn to defend oneself.

John Hemming, born 1931

Richard Brown's experiences were a frightening reality:

The very first day I went into training school I realised what I'd come into. I was sent to wait in the common room until the housemaster could see me. There were about three lads in there and they were playing table tennis. All of a sudden this lad came along, this little one and said, 'Can you play table tennis?' and I said 'yeah'. He said, 'Can you play against him?' and I said, 'yeah'. Of course I couldn't play – I don't think I scored a point! [So I said] 'Sorry about that' and he put the bat down and smack! Hit me! He knocked me out. When I came round … he said 'You said you could play'. I said 'I didn't!' 'Don't you argue with me!' I thought, 'That's a good introduction to the school. What have I come to?' There was a hell of a lot of violence. You knew your place. You were careful, extremely careful. You could get beaten up in the middle of the night, whenever there was an opportunity. On the one evening we went to bed and there was an absolute horrific scream. So horrific it was terrible. We looked out the windows and within a few minutes: 'ding ding ding ding' – police, ambulance, then we saw somebody being pulled out. By this time word had got round someone had poured acid into this kid's face in the middle of the night. They wanted to know where the acid came from. In those days the acid was in little bottles that were inside the triangular fire extinguishers. He'd taken these out and poured it in this kid's face! Everybody stole from everybody else. If it was there you stole it. I wouldn't have done that before. It was just an incidental thing. Teaching us how to do it. I learnt more from those people there – they taught me how to use wrong, as opposed to right from wrong. There is a vast difference.

Richard Brown, born 1941

A lot of people commit crime to fund their drugs habits. If you're going to spend £100 a day you're not going to do it by working legitimately, because you're not going to be able to hold a job down anyway. So you've got to go and burgle or break into cars to fund that habit. They're not getting that much money for it because the handlers they are selling them onto know they've got addictions and so they'll give them low amounts of money, which is obviously why they've to do more jobs to make the money.

Tina Dodd, born 1957

Drugs have become the scourge of the later years of the century. Karen talks frankly about her experiences:

Heroin came on the scene when I was about twenty. I got offered it, tried it once and found it really quite relaxing, and we used to go out clubbing often and, of a weekend, when you were feeling a bit frayed at the edges and coming down we used to often buy a little bit and 'toot' it (like chasing the dragon) on a Sunday. And that used to relax you and you'd come down so much easier. Then it became enjoyable and more appealing so we changed. Instead of going out clubbing all the time (we didn't have enough money) we'd go out and get some heroin instead. I started injecting as well …

Once you enter that circle you are always in touch and there's always numbers. If you can't get it from Droitwich, you can get it from Birmingham. If you can't get it from Birmingham you can get it from Worcester. People usually have a list of about ten phone numbers so you are always guaranteed to be able to get something. Maybe it's not at the beginning of the day. Maybe you have to wait but there's absolutely loads of heroin around. It's actually easier to get a bag of heroin than it was to get a £10 deal of cannabis. It's definitely grown to a massive extent and there's a lot, a lot in Droitwich, and there's a lot in Warndon, in Worcester. The amount of people it's increased to – at the start there was only so many people you knew, but now there's hundreds of people into it. There's still a lot who don't but it is more widely used now.

Karen, the gymnast, aged eleven.

It's just the availability of it. It's easy. I was probably addicted to it for about a year. By that time I'd lost my job and I was having to get money to get the heroin so I used to go with some friends and we used to go shoplifting. I had a car so I used to drive and we'd go to Birmingham and we'd go to places like Safeway's and the things that we stole were big coffee jars, 10lbs or something – just get about six or seven of those and sell them to people in pubs. And then we'd go to score and we couldn't wait until we got back to Droitwich and we'd take all our equipment with us and have [a] hit in Birmingham, in a car park, and that's how I used to feed my habit. I stole some money off my parents which was quite sad. I wasn't enjoying it anymore because I was waking up and I needed a hit and I had to run around all day shoplifting – and then get it – and it just became a horrible rigmarole. And I just thought, 'I've got to stop it now' because there were people I knew in the same circle who had just been there for seven, eight years and I thought to myself, 'One year is enough to lose – seven years is a good part of my life and I could end up dead'. So that's when I decided to go for help.

Karen, born 1972

Karen no longer takes drugs and is fully recovered. She is currently training to be a nurse.

CHAPTER 7
Growing up and getting older

Cynthia Pearson with her parents in 1940,
aged eighteen months.

Cynthia Pearson on holiday in Somerset.

How keeping the distance of a herring between you can be a successful contraceptive, and stories of boots with cardboard soles. The pros and cons of smoking oak leaves, and having the odd drop too much. People in Worcestershire discuss street games, family life, and losing their virginity. After the flush of youth has gone, there are stories of getting older from twins Cecily and Freda.

My mother always had the cane on the table by the side of her. So, if you put your hands on the table when you shouldn't do so you had a snap. 'Don't do that!' If you transgressed you were carted away from the table, you had to leave your meal, and they put you on the stairhead and closed the door. You soon had the discipline that you didn't do it again. She never showed any emotion. You see, this is the problem with a big family because there are so many of you – none of us got individual endearments. They never used to give us a cuddle or anything. They'd give you a slap and say, 'Oh, go on with you!' There was no kissing and cuddling like there is today. Well they couldn't go through the family like that. They couldn't make flesh of one and fowl of the other. You were all treated the same. You could tell there was emotion there but it was never brought out. They never showed it.

Ellis Wilson, born 1907

We children used to get together – we were a happy lot. We had gangs. I was the leader of the Edgar Street gang and Ernie Adams was the leader of the Severn Street gang. We used to get together and play games … silly games really. Someone had an old alarm clock. We used to put it on the pavement, wind it up and set it for five minutes or something, and the idea was you used to run like hell up Severn Street, down Edgar Street, round St. Peters Street, King Street, back up Sidbury, before the alarm went off. If you could do it that was a chalk mark on the wall.

Derrick Bollen, born 1917

We were poor. I remember my dad used to cut the Quaker Oats box up to put in my shoes to go to school with in the morning because I'd got holes in my shoes. If it was wet I didn't get very far before it was soaking wet and gone. We went to Franche School and there was a scheme whereby they had a police boot fund, and I was one of six children in the school that was chosen to be taken down to the police station to get a pair of boots and a jersey. I suppose that tells you I was one of the poorest children in the school at the time. It was the old Vicar Street police station. We were shepherded into this room – it was a small room – gas lit, and wooden boards on this floor. We had to try these boots on. They punched holes in the rear of the boots – I presume it was to stop parents selling them. I was pleased I'd

Left: Mike Edwards with his father and grandmother in 1932. *Right:* Bert Verity and brother, Bernie, in 1918.

70

got some shoes on my feet. It gave me a different sense of security. But they wore out like the rest of them!

Ron Jennings, born 1927

I did eventually have piano lessons. I found if I heard a tune I could immediately sit at the piano and play it by ear. Not properly but well enough and my mum decided she'd send me to piano lessons. I had to walk about two and a half miles every Saturday morning with this music case and I hated the lessons because I couldn't read the music and the teacher was very strict and seemed to spend [the] whole time rapping me across the knuckles with a ruler. In the end I think they gave up on me! There was one little girl came for her lesson just when I was finishing mine, and in disgust the music teacher pulled me off the stool and this little girl sat down and played the music beautifully and [the teacher] said, 'That's how you should be playing!' I sat back at the piano and immediately played this tune from memory just by ear. Of course, that wasn't acceptable. I think she had a quiet word with my mum and I don't remember going to music lessons again. That was the end of that!

Kathleen Robinson, born 1929

At the start of the century, the roadway was the natural place to play:

The roadway was perfectly clean and it was an ideal place for

Ted, Nellie, and Winnie Barber, ready for school in the early 1900s.

children to play – and with no motor traffic, nothing to harm a child. Occasionally there'd be a bicycle (but very seldom) and we would go out and draw a hopscotch bed on the pavement and play hopscotch. As children, we walked a mile up to school and then a mile home at dinner time, and then back again and then we walked home in the afternoon so all us children walked four miles a day. Then we'd be out playing in the evening – 'Tip Cat'. I thought it was because boys couldn't afford to buy cricket balls and cricket bats so they made these Tip Cats, which was a piece of wood sharpened at each end and then you had a bat

71

and you hit one of the points and it would shoot up into the air. When it was up in the air you got your bat and you'd hit it as hard as you could down the road. Then some children would have some whips and tops. We were experts with those as well. A whip, you'd wrap it round your top and pull it and the top would spin round and you'd hit it and it would go down the pavement and you'd go right down to the corner of the road and back hitting your top with your whip. Skipping, of course, we had a huge skipping rope – a piece of mother's old clothes line – it stretched from one side of the road to the other, one girl on one side and one on the other, turning it and we used to sing:
'All in together girls, never mind the weather girls,
I saw Esau, sitting on a see saw
Shoot, bang, fire!'
Then you'd run out of the rope and whoever got caught in it would have to turn the rope the next time.

Winifred Barber, born 1907

Times and values may have changed but the games were startlingly similar:

We didn't have much money but we used to use cigarette cards – that was the barter. From our bedroom window, if you stood on a chair, you could see into the bedrooms of the bed and breakfasts. On occasions you used to see people up there – ladies entertaining their men guests and vice versa, so for a cigarette card you could have five minutes on the chair! So we used to have a queue of little boys outside – to see what they could see in the bed and breakfasts.

Derrick Bolen, born 1917

And one must always try the forbidden fruit:

I've got a very good friend. His name is Arthur … I always remember, he'd got a cold frame. Arthur and I went and got some acorns from the garden and made some pipes so we could have a smoke. We got some dried oak leaves and ground them up into a powder, lifted the lid of the glass frame – and we both got into it and started smoking! My word we were sick and bad! When our mothers found out what we'd been doing we both had a caning.

Ellis Wilson, born 1907

The first time I ever got drunk was quite a wicked experience, actually! There was a girl in Clifton whose father made scrumpy cider and she used to bring bottles into the village and we'd just sit there drinking it, and I remember drinking absolutely loads and just bawling my eyes out all night and my mum and dad said, 'You're drunk!' But they thought it was quite funny. I must have been about eleven – so it wasn't as if I was an eight-year-old. The next morning I had the worst hangover and I did get a lecture, 'You shouldn't be drinking! You're not supposed to drink until you're eighteen!' But I took no notice.

Gavin Yarnold, born 1937

Left: The crowning of the May Queen, Pansy Austin, in 1934. *Right:* Pansy Austin and her brother, Sid, are pictured in Weston Super Mare, 1933.

Winifred Barber's school photograph of Kings Heath girls' school in the 1920s.

Sir Edward Elgar had Napleton Grange for a short while and I was about seven or eight at the time (and I used to deliver the paper there) and one sunny afternoon in the summertime he was sat underneath the horse chestnut tree and he was writing a score of music and as I went up the drive he shouted to me (I was on an old bicycle with no pedals!) and he shouted, 'Boy, bring it here'. So I took the paper over to him – it was the *Worcester Journal* (it was on a Friday) and *The Times* and I saw, on the score, and I'm pretty sure it was – he was writing Pomp and Circumstance – Land of Hope and Glory.

Ellis Wilson, born 1907

The Red Cross train arrived with the wounded soldiers:

There was a time when we only went to school part-time because in 1916 there was so many wounded, they filled all the hospitals and then they began looking round to find other buildings they could turn into hospitals, and they began looking at the schools. The school I went to was a Victorian school the boys were downstairs and the girls were upstairs. We were all very separate in those days – even the playground had a long wall in between it so the boys were on one side and we were on the other, but there was another school in our district that had been built only four or five years before the war started and

Lilly Peach, aged nine, learns to swim.

it was a single storey. Of course there were two buildings – one for boys and one for girls – and each had got a hall. The girls had got a lovely kitchen and the boys had got a big wood-working room. They looked at this school and thought that, for a hospital, [it] would be absolutely ideal, so the school that I belonged to had got to be used by both schools. One school would go in the morning and one in the afternoon. I remember the first lot of soldiers that came into that hospital – a whole crowd of us children – about eight of us said, 'Oh let's go down to the station and see the Red Cross train go through' so we raced down. It was so exciting! This train came in absolutely full of wounded soldiers – there was a lot of blood and that – they'd come straight from France and as soon as it stopped I shouted into this carriage, 'You're nearly there. It's only the next station'. And they began to cheer and all these children, they began running up the [platform] into each carriage shouting 'You're nearly there – it's only the next station' And as the train went out they were all cheering.

Winifred Barber, born 1907

If it was raining we couldn't go out for PT. There was the porch where all the coats and hats were and we would squeeze virtually the whole of the school in except the very little ones, and that's where we learned our tables. You all chanted them together, you know, 'Four fours a' sixteen, five fours a' twenty…', and you all finished up, 'Twelve twelves are a hundred and forty-four!' But it stuck with you. Today when I came back from up

north to do supply teaching in the area for a few years youngsters would say to me, 'We have the calculators don't we?' and I'd say 'You don't need those calculators!' 'Why not? We need them for our tables' and I'd say, 'Try me' and I'd go round and they'd say 'Nine nines?' and I'd go, 'Eighty-one' and they'd look at me as if I was a miracle man. But it all stemmed from this form of education.

Mike Edwards, born 1931

The early days of courting and marriage could be a little confusing. Sex education wasn't on the school timetable then:

When I started courting my wife, my father come to me – I was fourteen – 'Now' he said, 'I'm going to tell you something. You keep the distance of a herring between you and the girl and you will never come to any harm. But God help you if you get her into any trouble. Don't come back here – your clothes will be on the doorstep'. So, we never transgressed. I never transgressed. Of course, you had a cuddle and a kiss, one thing and another – when you were dancing you got close – but you always thought there was something else, you see, but you never knew quite what it was because you were never told anything as a child. And only a few years ago did I learn something about life that I never knew which would appertain to [being a] married couple! My wedding night – shall I tell you? We lay there and went to sleep! For three nights! I mean, we were so primitive in our

Mike Edwards is seen teaching in the late 1960s.

knowledge, we never resorted to what they do today.

Ellis Wilson, born 1907

But not so, now:

I lost my virginity at thirteen and I was quite open about it because I'm an open bloke and I told a few people – it went round the school. Because I'd done it, everybody else tried to do it so then suddenly there was this array of sex happening here and sex happening there and so-and-so slept with so-and-so. It was quite rife actually. It was more into the third and fourth years that this was going on and by the fifth year everybody had done it.

Gavin Yarnold, 1976

What my mother used to say to me was, 'If you don't want your fingers burnt, don't play with fire'. Now that was her way of giving me a sex education. She'd do very naive things like she'd say, 'We've always had animals'. So the fact you'd got some dog running about the kitchen was meant, in some way, to transmit all the facts of life to you! But in fairness I don't think they had the words or the understanding to do it. They obviously understood how sex worked but it wasn't talked about.

Bert Verity's wedding day was held at St John's church in Kidderminster, 1943.

There weren't magazines about. It's everywhere now, and very young children see things going on and understand – but it wasn't talked about and we certainly weren't prepared for what was to come. My husband-to-be gave me my sex education!

Cynthia Pearson, born 1938

People from Worcestershire discuss the pros and cons of getting older:

I got married during the war. I came home on leave and met the wife, by accident really. We decided to go out and we got married in 1943. I had a job to get the time off to get married. That was an episode. We had nowhere to stay, so someone gave us an address in Rhyl. We had to catch the train at a quarter to two. It didn't come in till four o'clock and we didn't get to Rhyl till midnight. In a thunderstorm! Then we found this house and it was a two-up and two-down and they'd gone to bed. Anyway, she came down and gave us a cup of cocoa. The next day we got up and we thought we'd go for a walk and there were thousands of soldiers going up and down the beach, training. It's been successful. We've been married fifty-four years now.

Bert Verity, born 1916

Cynthia Pearson in the 1950s.

Once I'd got over the shock of being on my own – life can be very lonely – you'd come home on a Friday night, walk up these steps and walk in here and think, 'What am I going to do now till Monday?' I can do things – you get in the car, you can go shopping or go to look at an exhibition somewhere, you go to visit somebody or invite somebody. But it's like you're in a play really because you're just doing things to pass the time and although I'm quite capable of doing that in my head I know I'm just passing the time and I wanted … I thought I wanted to share my life with somebody. How many men want a woman of sixty? They are all looking for something younger. So I just ploughed on. Then a friend of mine had been invited by a cousin to go and spend a week on his boat in Malta. I'd been to Malta and it was one of those places I'd decided I never ever wanted to go back to and she's not a very good sailor and she hates boats! We thought we were mad but we went! And it was lovely. Brian and Doreen met us from the plane and took us back to the boat and the next morning we were sitting on deck in the marina having our breakfast and I said casually to Doreen, 'He's such a nice man, Brian. How did you meet him?' And she said, 'Through Dateline' and I said, 'Oh, you didn't! What an extraordinary thing to do' and she said, 'It's not like you think. What you have to remember is all you are doing is agreeing to meet someone for a drink. You're not agreeing to anything else. And if you'd rather do that than sit at home watching Coronation Street and doing your knitting then that's what you do'. So I took my courage in both hands and joined Dateline! Well, I did meet

some extraordinary men! I'd be sitting somewhere looking at my watch surreptitiously, thinking 'How much longer have I got to sit here politely before I can go?' I mean some of them were really, really boring. Then I agreed to meet this man. We met in a very nice hotel and although I'd been quite entertained by him I didn't think it would go any further. Anyway he rang again and he came here, then he invited me to his house and I nearly died! Outdoor floodlit swimming pool, big gym, a room as big as this whole house that was his billiard room – everywhere was immaculate and I thought – 'I feel like sixteen'. And I really did. Exactly like you would feel as a young girl, only this time there's no mother to censor me, I am not going to get pregnant because I am too old, and I have my own front door and suddenly the liberating affect of that was amazing. We had such fun. It was a really good time. Now it came to an end after two years but it was an amazing two years and it taught me a lot and it gave me a lot of confidence and it gave me my 'self' back, and I suddenly felt like a real person for the first time in my life. It was wonderful. I shall be forever grateful for that.

Cynthia Pearson, born 1938

Twins Cecily and Freda share a house, and some pastimes:

Freda: when I was sixty I made a positive decision to give up driving because I work on an orthopaedic ward, and I saw so many accidents caused by silly old fools driving I decided I wouldn't join them. Now that I'm sixty-seven I'm very pleased that I made that decision because people usually cling onto their cars until they are really not capable or fit to be driving. And they've got no alternative. But now I'm used to public transport, I'm used to my bicycle.

Cecily: when you start (at sixty) going for cycling holidays on your bicycle it's a bit unusual – for us, anyway, but we loved it. Two grey-haired ladies on bicycles, one carrying a set of 'bones' to play, to join in any music. We were just fêted all round, totally made a fuss of ... there's nothing brave about getting on a bicycle or camping on a campsite. There's nothing brave about going to another country and doing exactly the same! I look old. And of course I only have to look at Freda to see how old I look and I look older than she does. If I see my reflection in a shop window I think, 'Who is that old biddy?' And then I realise it's me. But I don't feel like that old biddy in the window. Do you know – I haven't done half of it yet. There are so many things I want to do. I know I won't have time. I don't want to be old,

Freda: I want to pop my clogs when I'm seventy. I don't want to be old and in hospital and I know the population is ageing all the time. The hospital service is going down all the time. People's bodies don't improve with age. People's brains don't improve with age. I don't want to hang about, thank you very much.

Cecily Lambourne and Freda Dutton, born 1932

The home of Robert Bell, Titton Hill Farm, in the 1900s.

An evocative poem from Mike Edwards to set the scene:

We called it automation
      Three horse hoes not just one
Hooked to the Fergie's tool bar
Because our Tommy's gone

We called it automation
Though four fellows, not just one
Were needed for the team now
Because our Tommy's gone

We called it automation
For when all was said and done
No need to rest a tractor
Now that our Tommy's gone

We called it automation
And we didn't stop to talk
To something with an engine
Turning wheels and not a walk

There's no need to brush the flies off
From the sweating heaving flanks
Because a tractor doesn't have them
Only fuel containing tanks

There's no need to stand and whistle
While it spreads its hind wheels wide
Because it shouldn't lose its water
In a running frothing tide

There's no need to stroke its muzzle
Or to gently pull its ears
Because a tractor doesn't have them
Just a choice of different gears

Oh, we called it automation
And we praised our new God, speed
But I wonder if a tractor
Does supply our every need?

Mike Edwards, born 1931

The onset of technology on the farm has changed the face of the landscape and farming forever. We look back on the days of the horse-drawn plough and the gypsy wagons with the itinerant workers with nostalgia. But it's good to remember how hard the work was – cherry tomatoes and picking sprouts, chemicals and asbestos. Farming in Worcestershire comes in for some scrutiny. Are the changes for the better?

During the war years we began to see lease-lend tractors coming over from America and they were the revolutionary piece of mechanism of the age because they had three-point linkage. Now, in the old days all your equipment was trailer equipment. You trailed it behind you. You'd got a trip out whether it was a plough or a scuffle or a skim before you got to the end of the land in order you could turn round. With the three-point linkage you simply pulled a lever and it came straight up so there were virtually no headlands needed.

Mike Edwards, born 1931

The wife came in with this bit of green stuff and I thought, 'I can do better than that!' I walked across these allotments and this chap said, 'You can have half this one here, I'm giving it up next year – the war's over.' So, I said, 'Can I borrow your spade?' and I started digging straight away. I grew everything. I had a good inclination on the farm of how things went. Rotation is the thing – this was an old farming method. Today they plant corn twice but they didn't then. I don't use a lot of

Bert Verity as a boy, feeding the lambs at Church Farm, Shrawley.

sprays. The apples and cherries and plums that used to be in the country was beautiful – today they look beautiful in the shops but they haven't got the taste. You miss that. You miss the smell of the hay, and those big elm trees have just disappeared.

Bert Verity, born 1916

Mechanisation was our biggest change. We had an old second-hand Fordson tractor just before the war and I had learned to drive it. The Fordson was then a motor horse, rather than a tractor as they are today. We had a wonderful old waggoner, and he came back. He'd been retired before the war and he came back to help. And one of the things – he was a very good ploughman with a horse, and I was driving the tractor and he taught me how to plough and particularly on

sloping ground, which is always the difficult one. I'd always remember, we'd finished a particularly difficult field and I said, 'What do you think about the tractor?' 'Well,' he said, 'There's one thing it can't do, it can't shit!' Such a profound remark – it was wonderful because we were so reliant on getting as much muck into the land as we could. In the winter the waggoner used to go to Hartlebury station, day in and day out, weather come what may, to get loads of muck that was sent by rail from the Black Country. I remember those days well.

Robert Bell, born 1911

We'd come down here in the first week in May. You'd start picking the peas in June, after Bromsgrove Fair. There was never no early stuff like there is now. You wouldn't be picking stick

83

Robert Bell, following the binder at Titton Hill Farm.

Lilly Peach helping with the lambs.

beans in the middle of July, it was always August. We pick the peas, then we'd go off the peas onto the ground beans, and you'd pick them in pea nets. After you finished those you'd go on to the broad beans in 100cwt sacks and you'd pick them, a shilling a bag. If you earned a pound in them, you'd think you'd got yourself a millionaire. Not like it is today. We used to do the beetroot a shilling a cwt. Get it off the ground, screw it and bag it and weigh it. We used to do all that for a shilling. We'd all help one another. Through the run of the day the family would earn about £4. Even the little 'uns would help. We used to work for all the farmers round Pershore, Evesham. We used to pick the hops in a crib, a shilling a bushel. I worked on the top of Holt Fleet for an old Welsh chap – his language was wicked! My eldest daughter used to cut the binds. That was from half past six in the morning till half past six at night. She went in a half-hour earlier than me and finished a half-hour earlier. When you picked them your hands would be stained and what a nasty smell! You could wash your clothes over and over but they always smelt of hops. It weren't a very good job when it was wet, not very nice at all – you'd get soaked. And the mud up and down the fields – we used to do a bit of cussing about that, tell you the truth.

Harriet Hall, born 1922

If you started in January, your main crop was going to be sprouts. Then as you came into the spring, you would start of by cutting winter lettuce then there would be

This asparagus, seen on the Edwards farm, was part of the 'Gras' show.

Left: Fred Mumford and Len Edwards cutting lettuce in the 1930s.

cauliflowers, which had over-wintered in pots in the greenhouse and had been planted out, March time. As you came up to the end of April, depending on how warm the season was, you would find asparagus was gradually coming in. So in the height of the summer, you would be cauliflower-cutting, lettuce-cutting, asparagus-cutting, beetroot would be coming in, then there would be various carrot crops. Then you would be coming through to late summer – autumn cauliflowers, the planting of spring cabbage, and then you were back round into the sprouts. If anybody said to me, 'Of all the jobs you ever do, which was the worst?' I think I would say, 'Sprout topping on a frosty morning!'

Mike Edwards, born 1931

Richard Clay remembers the cattle market in Worcester in the early part of the century:

On a Monday, which was market day in Worcester, I should think about six or eight flocks of sheep (of about fifty or sixty) came in, plus two dogs and two boys. They spread all over the road and they just walked their way slowly up the road, flock after flock, all interspersed with cattle. There wasn't much traffic, and it had to get through as best as it could. I always felt sorry for the calves – they were taken in a float with a net over the top, and the poor cow had to weave her way behind. Then, you saw the mother coming back without the calf. It was rather sad that. [The sheep and cattle] walked all the way down to the market from I don't know where and then, poor beggars, they walked all the way back in the afternoon. I know one occasion with the cattle when two of the herds got muddled and one man was short by one cow. I don't know how they sorted it out. They were still arguing at dusk!

Richard Clay, born 1905

He [my grandfather] had everything. Fruit, vegetables, he even had a coal business! He used to sell timber, cattle – he'd got three farms then. He was a wealthy man but if you worked for him, you didn't get any favours. When I started (I left school just before I was fourteen) it was 7s 6d for a fifty-two-hour week. My first job was to get a horse and go up and down the fields, harrowing. That was my first paid day. You'd do eleven or twelve miles a day walking. He used to sell lorry loads of stuff on the Wolverhampton market and he used to buy the other people's stuff as well. I remember the first tractor – a little old Fordson tractor. I liked the tractors. They used to let me have a go when I was fourteen.

Bert Verity, born 1916

We all employed a lot of people, certainly up until the 1920s. Farming was in a very poor state then. My father came here in 1909 and there was a slight boom, because of the war and the necessity for food, so farming had a little surge. Then it went right back – and it is in a very bad state now. We were a close-knit community. My father was very forward thinking. He came in from the Manchester area and had nothing to do with farming – it was just his desire to be on the land. I think he treated his staff in an entirely different way to others. It was common policy, almost in lieu of wages, to give the workers drink, cider. Almost every farm grew a few cider and perry pears. In our cellar we had hogsheads of cider. My father disagreed with this method entirely and he was one of the first to stop [giving cider as wages].

Robert Bell, born 1911

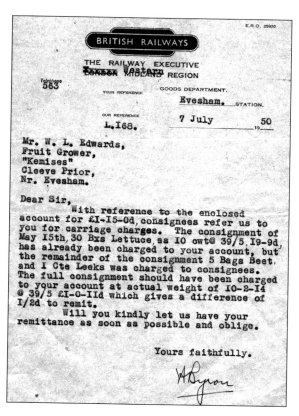

These carriage charges date from 1950.

It was frightening that new substances had arrived on the market, but there were no health warnings attached:

If you take the advances in science, which a war will bring about, and you consider advances in science which help you to win that war, you tend to trust the scientists. It's going to be the 'Brave New World'. We used mercuric chloride in which to dip cauliflower plants against wire stem. We never thought of putting gloves on, we never thought whether we'd got cuts or chaps on our hands, you know, you plunge you hands into tubs, you never gave it a thought! We put up a Dutch greenhouse. What do we use? Asbestos. Asbestos came in sheets which was twice as wide as we wanted, so we'd got a circular saw in one of the outbuildings and we simply put the asbestos in the circular saw! All these various things – there just was not the awareness.

Mike Edwards, born 1931

There is no use for soil for the modern growers:

This is a half-acre block of modern Venlow Dutch glasshouse that is housing cherry tomatoes which are our main crop – they are about eight foot tall, probably two weeks away from harvest. None of our crops are grown in the soil now. The organic people moan like hell about that but this particular block is grown in recirculated solution. It's computer controlled, the environment, the water, the heating, the humidity, the carbon dioxide. That's how it has to be grown these days.

From the time I can remember there was small amounts of old-type glass structures, and tomatoes would have been grown in the soil. We would have many root-born diseases, corky root was the main one, so people used to have to sterilise the ground. That was done, traditionally, with steam. You cooked the ground with steam. There's various methods but they used to use a steam plough and it was pulled very slowly through the ground with steam being injected at the same time. Then another way was fork steaming. That was very labour intensive. You had a series of forks, again with holes in for the steam to come out. You'd cook an area ten foot square for maybe eight hours – so you can see it took an awful long time to cover a large area. Steaming became unpopular, because in the late '70s, fuel became exceptionally expensive. Therefore, cooking the ground with steam was a very expensive method, so the first growing method after soil was peat. Even in peat, the roots would become infected. The next development was rock-wool, which is the same as the loft insulation you see. It's probably a lot warmer than peat was, so that is now the industry's standard growing media.

The computer runs and monitors all three greenhouses. If you turn the screen on we have an overview of the day conditions – we've got an outside temperature, wind speed and wind direction and a light sum. The light sum is a very important feature because it's on that we initiate a lot of conditions for the crop. If it's a bright day we might ask the crop to be grown warmer. If it's a dull day, we might cool the night down. We can override the computer but it's really like sucking your finger, putting it in the air, and saying, 'Have we got it right?' We could not grow the crop without it.

Paul Drew, born 1956

To walk into a stable of horses in the morning it was alive, it was pulsating, and they'd stop chewing – 'Oh, he's here again'. So different to going into a cold tractor shed. There was life there, there was life in the animals. The boss used to say, 'We are going muck hauling today'. We'd go into a fold yard which was probably four feet deep in muck, cut it out in chunks, put it onto carts, take it down to the fields and dump it. But those were all jobs. They'd look at us today and say, 'However did they do it?' But those were all jobs – without forklift trucks, without JCBs, but we did it.

John Drew, born 1928

And to finish, the days of 'Pick Your Own' were on their way up, and Robert Bell made the most of them:

I saw the opportunity – I began to open our fields to the public. I adopted a policy of letting them come in and take

'Pick Your Own' t Titton Hill, 980s.

'Pick Your Own' at Robert Bell's Titton Hill Farm, 1980s.

the best. Well, it was absolutely phenomenal. The money just rolled in and I think within three years we'd more or less got rid of the overdraft. It was the right time. The public had never seen such wonderful fruit and the roads round here were blocked at the weekend. I have had to go to the corner of the main road and stop people coming in. It lasted at least ten years.

Robert Bell, born 1911

Robert branched out into other types of fruit but the last straw(berry?) came with the cream and sugar!

Then we developed into a farm shop and we were open seven days a week. The glamour has gone now. It was beginning to go in 1985. The public were less enamoured of it and the shop [turnover] was increasing. The amount of policing we had to do got more and more because we were having an awful lot of pilfering. People would come here at the weekend for a feed. We've seen them come here with their own sugar and cream and eat them in the fields!

Robert Bell, born 1911

CHAPTER 9

Food

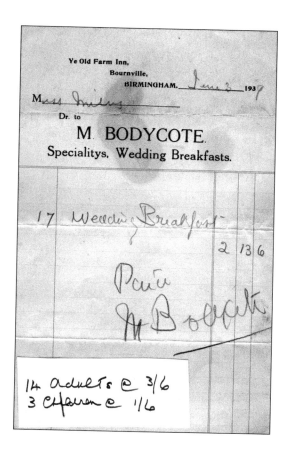

This bill was for Winifred Barber's wedding
breakfast, which included meat, salads, pickles,
bread rolls and cream trifle.

Organic pork, old-fashioned bread and doorstep delivery by the baker with a horse and cart. Stories from behind the scenes in the restaurant and the children who worked in the ice cream business, plus the butcher who swapped a ham for some 'indigestion powder that goes in tea!'

The traditional co-op:

The Sidbury Co-op has never been altered – not the outside. But inside of course was the long counter, behind the counter were little tiny drawers and on the outside it used to say 'Pepper', not salt. They used to sell salt in blocks but there was pepper, tea, caraway seeds, nutmegs – anything like that – all labeled on the outside. Now at the bottom there was the make-up counter. That was where the sugar used to come in sacks and used to be weighed up, and on the right hand side going on was the provision counter, and normally two men, Nipper and Cyril, used to serve the provisions. Gwen Hayward used to look after the cake counter and she used to take pity on me on a Saturday if I was working all day. If there was any cake left – they used to have slabs of cake and they used to cut it and weigh it – any ends left she used to put them in a bit of paper and give them me to eat.

Derrick Bollen, born 1917

Winifred Barber remembers fresh baked bread with the odd added horse hair:

Sometimes when he got by us, the baker would get off his cart and decide it was time to give the horse some food. And he'd get the big bag and put it over its neck and head and he'd pat the horse and get up on his cart and get the basket and lift the loaves out with his hands. There was no washing of hands. We must have swallowed millions of germs! The loaves were unwrapped and unsliced … tin loaves and cottage loaves and bloomers and little batches. He knew what every household wanted. We didn't have any brown bread in the week. My mother always bought a brown loaf for tea on a Sunday – we always had brown bread and butter. And Christmas time, a birthday party – she'd buy a brown loaf but we didn't have brown for general use and I don't remember any wholemeal at all. It was all just white bread.

Winifred Barber, born 1907

Of course, bread kept a long time – very different from what it does today … they put something in it and it preserved it. You could save crusts off the bread for a month and they wouldn't go mouldy. They'd just go hard. My mother used to save all her crusts and make a great big bread pudding, put eggs in it, raisins, sultanas. She'd got a great big meat dish and she'd make the bread pudding every week and it was kept on the cold slab, and when we came home from school if we felt hungry we could always go and cut a big chunk of bread pudding and take it in the garden and eat it. We ate dozens and dozens of bread puddings. It was one of the things my mother always had as a standby.

Winifred Barber, born 1907

'Tiger' Taylor was a local pig-killer and boatman.

Rabbit was often on the menu, with the occasional pheasant:

It would be better for me than quite a few of the villagers because my father used to catch quite a lot of rabbits. He used to do quite a lot of shooting. He taught me to shoot and we used to supply the village with rabbits in the war. I've known a time when I've had to skin and dress as many as thirty rabbits on a Sunday night in the old zinc bath. The people used to come and say, 'Mr Bird, have you got any rabbits?' 'Yes, which would you like? One that I caught in a net, or one that I shot?' The ones that you caught in a net were dearer than the ones you shot. In those days you had to save the skin because the rag-and-bone man used to come round and you used to get a penny for the skins, and they used to sell these skins to make fur gloves. As I say, we were lucky in as much we'd have two or three rabbits in the week, or pigeons. Sometimes it was pheasants! I mean if there was a pheasant about, my father got it like.

That was it!

Francis Bird, born 1926

I didn't even know what a chicken was when I was young. All we had was rabbit. Rabbit stew. A great big black pot used to hang over the fire – no gas or electric fires in those days, it was all open fires. That used to go on for about three days, dipping your bread in. That's all we had to live on really. Sometimes there was no food on the table. You imagine a woman having thirteen children, hardly any money, and then she had to feed her brood and sometimes we went to bed, my brother and I, and we always clung to each other. We'd sit on the step and wait for

Pansy Austin feeding the pig in 1929.

my mum to come home at ten o'clock at night. She'd have a loaf of bread in her pack. It was very hard in those days. Not like today. In those days you'd go down the Shambles, and they'd auction it off about ten o'clock at night, that's when she used to get some steak. A couple of bob, a nice piece of meat – we used to tuck into that! But mainly, bread and lard for dinner. There again, we survived!

Cath Wild, born 1929

The way to cook a pig:

The butcher would come down and kill the pig humanely and then he'd put it in the fire … they used to cover him over with straw and set fire to him, burn all the hair off it, then scrape it, then put it on the bench, dress it like. That's how they use to do it. You couldn't do it today, they wouldn't allow you to – health and safety – but nobody was ever ill. You didn't have it all yourself. Everybody used to have a piece … people used to use every part of the pig. We had an old wash house and we used to hang the pig up in the wash house in two halves … then you used to have to cure the pig before you could do what you wanted with it.

Francis Bird, born 1926

The sides were put on the pig bench in the back kitchen and they were salted. The salt was rubbed in. Mum used to seem to know exactly where the veins were. She'd start in the middle, press with her thumb, go in all different directions and when she come to the outside, to the cut part, the blood would come out of the end of the vein. If you could take the blood out there was less chance of anything going bad. The bacon was turned about once a week. We had bacon and egg every morning for breakfast. What they'd think of it now. All that fat. I'm seventy-one [and] all three of my brothers are all going strong. It couldn't have done us any harm.

Pansy Austin, born 1927

Preserving the food didn't seem to present much of a problem:

We didn't have a fridge until I had been married twenty-five years. I managed with the stone slab in the pantry. All the houses had pantries ... the top shelf in the pantry would be full of jars of jam by the autumn, ready for all through the winter and the spring. And we grew a lot of kidney beans. We put them in salt. We'd got big jars we used to put them in whole. We didn't cut them up, just take the sides off and put them into salt and leave them and they were nice to eat. Tureens we'd use, because there was no plastic at all till after the First World War. It was all crock, glass jars. Sometimes you see these jars of sweets in shops. Some people would get those and they would hold quite a lot of beans.

Winifred Barber, born 1907

Before cellophane and cling film:

We saved all the big jars we could and mum would buy some mutton fat from the butcher because mutton fat, when it sets, it sets hard. We'd gently stew the fruit in syrup, put it in the jars, leave a good inch at the top of the jar, render this mutton fat down so that it was liquid and fill the top of the jar up with that, put a bit of paper on the top and seal it down with more paper (greaseproof paper) and a bit of string and although the top of the fat went a bit mouldy, months later when you cut that, the stuff underneath was perfect.

Pansy Austin, born 1927

Ron Jennings remembers the family ice cream business, with some resentment!

Dad got a friend who gave him a recipe for ice cream in the early '20s and that was hard work. When we came on the scene, the ice cream business was there. The ice had to be fetched from Kidderminster – Dixon Street the ice works was – and [we] were school age and we'd have to fetch this ice from Kidderminster and the means of transport was a plank with two wheels at either end. Sounds incredible but that's what we used to do ... take it with a couple of hessian sacks. It was a round trip of about six miles. It used to take us hours to do this! By the time we got back, the hundred weight of ice would be considerably lighter! We did it for years, once a week in the summer every Saturday morning. I hated it.

Ron Jennings, born 1927

Vegetarianism is growing. You've got to cater for vegetarians and vegans. Whereas in the '70s a vegetarian would have a cheese salad or an omelette and be called a freak, now, it's endless. Spinach and mushroom pancakes, vegetable bakes and lots of things. I enjoy catering for them. You're surprised when you try it – it's quite nice really. There are always two vegetarian alternatives on our menu. [The beef scare] was a major one. We still cooked beef and let people make their own decision about whether they ate it. At first there were a few hardened beef eaters that weren't going to change. But a lot of people did. I think a lot of people still don't eat it. Roast beef on a Sunday isn't as popular as it used to be before that, so we always do three roasts on a Sunday so people can make the choice.

Robin MacAllistair, born 1957

Ron Jennings went to work in his uncle's butchers shop:

The war was on. Everything was rationed. I used to ride a carrier bike with a big basket on the front and one day he got a big ham, wrapped it in his butchers apron, put it in the basket and said, 'Now, you take that up to Mr Dunn (which was the bakers) and you tell Mr Dunn I've brought you this and I'd like a half hundredweight of indigestion powder that goes in tea!' Which was obviously sugar! So he'd

swapped the ham for sugar! That's what they used to do in those days. Illegal, I suppose!

Ron Jennings, born 1927

Iain Patton started his own business recently, supplying 'Happy Meat':

I'd been vegetarian for many years. I'm not sentimental about eating meat as long as it has been treated well, and I feel animals can be treated well. More and more what goes into the meat is an issue – steroids, hormones, growth promoters – and because I was feeding very basic meal and vegetable scraps I knew these pigs had a good life and weren't full of chemicals. It's terrible what has gone on post-war, and farming is still in that trap. I do not blame the farmers … but the funding mechanisms and the supermarkets which they rely on has really become the stranglehold on them, and things have to change and are changing, in my view for the better. And I can recognise British farming is starting to grasp the nettle of welfare and reduced dependence on fertilizers and pesticides. Organic food will take off in the next five to ten years and more and more farmers are … saying this is where the future is and the prices will come down. Looking at our own 'Happy Meat' customers, we are getting a wider spread. I have got four sows and sixty-five sheep. We are tiny and we aren't going to be supplying supermarkets so [we are] safe in the knowledge we are going to supply a local market. Given that I feel people in this area are more concerned about welfare and the quality of the food, I

Iain Patton with Hilda, an old spot sow, 1990s.

feel relatively confident.

Iain Patton, born 1966

To finish – family mealtimes:

We talked at mealtimes. There were seven of us and with some out at work we didn't always get to the table together but when we did there was always quite a lot of conversation, and problems were ironed out. If there were any upsets, my oldest brother used to try and settle them for us. You don't think of it at the time but afterwards you realise it helped to formulate your views and grow up and know who you were. I think so few children have that now – that's perhaps something that's a great tragedy.

Tony Baxter, born 1909

The mealtime was a family time when you got together, exchanged news, discussed anything that was important, made sure everybody knew if they'd got a dental appointment or whatever. They were the times when everybody put their ha'pworth in and everybody knew what everybody was doing. Very important …that was the time when you said, 'Andrew, you've got to be at such-and-such for a certain time'. It was the daily timetable really. Now meals are far more snacks than proper meals. They can be taken anywhere, at any time. Get on a bus, people will be munching, anywhere you go, jaws are on the move. It wasn't necessary in the old days. We had three good meals a day and we did not eat in between.

Margot Beard, born 1912

97

CHAPTER 10
Playtime

Tony Baxter in 1937.

From the first moving pictures, kipper parties, charity balls and playing the saxophone – to the Manic Street Preachers, Afghan coats and chemical 'highs'. And then there's the tale of the forgotten knickers! Worcestershire people reveal what they do for entertainment:

A visit to the pictures was very special:

One day my brother came home from school, we were sitting at the table and he said, 'The boys at school are talking about moving pictures in the Institute on Saturday afternoon'. So I said 'Moving pictures? Can we go?' and he said, 'We'll ask mum'. And she said, 'Oh my dears, I don't think you could see moving pictures but if you want to go you can'. So on Saturday afternoon we raced off to the institute and it was crowded with children … and at last they opened the door and we went in and we paid our penny. We got into about the sixth row and this fellow came and he stood in front and he said, 'Now you're all going to see something this afternoon that you'll remember all the days of your life!' The lights went down and a light came onto the screen and the soldiers, the guardsmen on horseback started galloping along the front of the screen and all these children started shouting, 'They're moving, they're moving!' They were so excited they stood up, and everybody was screaming and shouting. They threw their caps up into the air and I can remember seeing the screen and seeing the shadow of all these caps coming down. And then we saw in the distance the Royal Coach coming. It was coming from a long distance and very slowly it came nearer and nearer until you could see Queen Mary and King George V sitting inside, and Queen Mary was lifting her hand up and the children were shouting, 'It's the Queen, it's the Queen!' And this coach came nearer and nearer until it got right to the edge of the screen and these children in the front row all got up and screamed and ran because they felt this coach was coming on top of them. You didn't realise it was only a picture … this really looked as if it was coming off the screen onto us!

Winifred Barber, born 1907

It was a treat … you couldn't often afford to go. A friend of mine at school had said that this girl had taken a shine to me. She wanted me to take her to the pictures on Saturday. I thought, 'It's going to cost me fourpence – where am I going to get that from?' The only thing I could think was to get hold of some rabbit skins because you could be paid tuppence at the rag-and-bone stall for these. So I got hold of a couple of skins from neighbours so I'd got my fourpence to take me into the picture house. I met this girl outside and we went in and we saw this film about Pearl White and it was absolutely wonderful and the train came down and the hero came galloping up and rescued her from the train line and everybody got so excited. These were the times the film on the screen was spattered with flashes and goodness knows what. But it was wonderful, it really was!

Bert Batty, born 1908

QUEENSWOOD
FOOTBALL DINNER 1928.

Menu

Native Oysters
Hors d'oeuvres

Thick Ox Tail
Clear Julienne

Boiled Turbot. Shrimp Sauce.

Roast Saddle of Mutton. Red Currant Jelly
Roast & Boiled Potatoes.
Cauliflower & Brocolli Tops.

Fricassee of Chicken.
Mashed Potatoes & Green Peas.

Fruit Jellies
Ice Pudding

Dessert

Coffee

This was the menu for the Queenswood Football Dinner in 1928.

We tried to persuade my father to go but he said it was a waste of time, they couldn't possibly make pictures move, but anyway we persuaded [him]. On the Saturday afternoon we said, 'Oh Dad, do come with us' and he said, 'Oh alright, I'll come'. We were a bit further back this time, probably in the twelfth row, and we were on a bench, my father sat in the middle, my brother on one side and me on the other. The soldiers started coming, marching with their big guns, and my father just sat there staring at the screen. He didn't move to right, to left. His face was just set and we kept looking at him and Ted kept saying, 'They are moving aren't they Dad? We were right weren't we Dad?' And all he kept saying was, 'Yes, yes'. We got home and he went up to my mother and he put his arm round her and he said, 'Lass, I've seen a miracle this afternoon'. 'Oh' she said, 'The children were right then'. 'Yes' he said, 'How they do it, I do not know, but they certainly move'.

Winifred Barber, born 1907

The canteen of Millwards factory was turned over to us on a Saturday night as our dance hall – our Mecca, you see. The boys seemed to gather round on the outside and the girls were sat around and in the early part of the time we had to have a card to pick our partners in the old-fashioned way (as we thought then). But that went out of the window very soon. We would look around and we would look for the likely lasses. But it was a great occasion and there was this globe in the middle of the room swinging round and on a Gala night we were all given packets of streamers to throw around. It was a wonderful thing.

Bert Batty, born 1908

Margot Beard had her own fish to fry:

Kipper picnics happened at night. Everybody was armed with kippers and sticks. There was generally a farmer involved because we would require a field, and the farmer would have obligingly put a fire ready for us or we would find kindling and make a fire. And when the fire was going well, there would be lots of beer (but it would be in bottles not cans) and we would hang our kippers on the ends of our sticks and dangle them over the fire until they were cooked or fell in the fire! It was just another way of amusing ourselves.

Margot Beard, born 1912

Jim Beechey into showbiz:

I thought I'd see if I could make a living playing the saxophone – which I did for a time. We started our own band, the Beechey Band, and that was in the '30s. We used to play all round Worcester. We played at the Britannia Hall every other Saturday, and we used to go to Droitwich – all round different places, playing. I put an advert in *The Stage* and the *Melody Maker*, telling them how good I was! It's no good putting in you aren't any good is it? 'First-class vocalist, tenor sax, clarinet, drums, requires summer season'. Anyway, I had several replies and one was offering me an audition in London and in those days it was a big jump from a little backwater. He offered me the job. It was up to thirty hours a week I think, at £4 a week. So, we high tailed it to Ramsgate, to the Marina Gardens. It was a big adventure.

Jim Beechey, born 1908

A glimpse of ankle in the 1920s:

The Charleston was absolutely brilliant. Girls were flappers that went to dances then. They could kick their legs up and we saw more than the

The roundabout.

A fancy dress event in 1959.

calf of their leg then. It was all brilliant, it was exhilarating! They didn't have any breasts in those days 'cos they had these long straight dresses with the waist nearly down to their backsides and so the picture was quite flat. The one important thing was we were now being able to see girls with frocks up to their knees. Only a few years before that, all the dresses were ankle length and to see a girl's calves – and some very shapely calves – it really got the blood flowing!

Bert Batty, born 1908

I knew how to dance because my brother Ted could dance. We danced round our sitting room. He could do the Charleston – oh, he was smashing with the Charleston. I said to my mother, 'Alice and her friends, they're all going to a dance at the Institute on Saturday. Could I go?' She said, 'Of course you can, love, but you'll need a dress won't you?' And my sister said she'd got a

pattern and she'd make me a dress, so Mother went to town and she bought some sateen. My sister made it – and I'd never had a dress without sleeves. I thought I was wonderful in this dress! Dear, dear! It was only pink sateen but I did think it was wonderful and Mother had bought me a pair of white dance shoes.

There was dancing everywhere. In the summertime they had dancing in the park. The bands would be there in the bandstand and then there'd be a big enclosure and you could go in there, and you'd dance and dance all Saturday. The park would be full of people. It was all very sociable, everybody was very happy. You met all your friends and you laughed and danced. Oh, I did think it was wonderful.

Winifred Barber, born 1907

The 'Monkey Run' and how to 'click' is explained:

On Sunday nights there was nothing for anyone to do. We lads used to gather together on the corner of the town, meeting to talk about how the football went on the day before, how the 'Baggies' had got on and how the 'Villa' had fared. Of course we talked about the lasses we'd met at the dance the night before. The girls would have been going to Sunday school, to evening classes and to church and so on, and they would come along to the Monkey Run from all ends of the town. It was a question of us all walking up and down the High Street – or what we called Evesham Street in those days. For the lads, if you hadn't 'clicked' by the time you got up to the Congregational church at the top of the town you were a no-hoper. And the girls were on a predatory prowl just as much as we

Jim Beechey and his wife in Ramsgate, 1939.

Mary Beattie (front left) was dressed as a snowball at this dancing class.

were. Evesham Street on Sunday night was crowded with all of us from all ends of the town looking to 'click'. Having walked up and down a bit, we would corral a group of girls into a shop window – a little bit of slap and tickle took place. If you were lucky you'd picked a good girl. If you hadn't and you'd picked a scrubber, you very quickly dropped her and were back to the Monkey Run for another pick.

Bert Batty, born 1908

Fashions were changing fast:

In the '50s, fashions were changing so fast, and attitudes and of course morals as well, because you were

Mary Macdiarmid is pictured at her home in Trinidad at carnival time in 1954.

approaching the pill coming in. You lived to go out. You went to work, you did your job. You came home and by gum you'd got to go out. You'd got to go to this dance, to that dance and you'd got to do as much as you could cram in. You tried to copy these stars, and Bill Haley had kiss curls and I bought a pink one and pinned this kiss curl [on]. Whatever I must have looked like, goodness only knows! And then of course the great high heels. The winkle-pickers which absolutely creased your feet. Unbelievable. Every week you had to take those shoes to be mended because the tips came off the end and you'd be walking about and you'd hear this clink-clonk, clink-clonk and into the cobblers: 'Can you get them done for Saturday?' They were prize shoes. We did have a lot of fun.

Jean Nichols, born 1940

We called it 'Bop'. It's called all sorts of different things – 'Jive' and whatever – but we called it 'Bop' and we used to have to have our 'boppers' which were these special flat 'bopping' shoes, and you went to the Bata shoe shop and you bought these pumps, and your vanity case, and you took your 'boppers' in your vanity case and you were tripping along in your great big high heel shoes and when you got to the dance you did your 'bopping' in your 'boppers'. Now, I'm in a flared, full circular taffeta skirt – and you used to wear the very full underskirts and when you 'bopped' and you spun round these skirts went round with you and this very nice RAF man came up. Very tall and started to 'Bop' straight away – this was wonderful. I was having the time of my life. You didn't stop for anything. You didn't stop to go to the lavatory, or to go for a drink. Then they had break halfway through. [I went] into the toilets – I'm in there, and I let out one almighty scream – I had not got any knickers on! My friend believed I'm the only person in the whole of this land that could go to an RAF camp full of 800 men, 'Bop' for an hour and a half with no knickers on!

Jean Nichols, born 1940

The make-up was white lipstick which was ghastly! And foundation (Max Factor pan stick) and you caked it on – thick liquid in a stick like a large lipstick. You also had to pluck your eyebrows so you virtually had no eyebrows left at all, and then you'd paint them back in a very surprised-looking arch as if someone had just given you a really nasty shock. The fashions had changed and we started to get into the '70s which was rather more glamorous than the '60s with the glittery clothes and the big platform soles and heels.

The boys wouldn't want to dance till the end of the evening. They'd stand around with their backs to the wall trying to brazen the whole thing out and get up enough courage to move in and ask someone to dance, usually for the last two records which would be slow ones! I'd got much more into the Rolling Stones by then. My mother didn't like them at all. There was a photo of them in the newspaper, but my cousin's wife brought this paper and showed it to my grandmother and said, 'See these? He murdered his own grandmother!' And my grandmother

believed it. She thought they were so rough and nasty looking and my mother thought they were disgusting as well. I think that was half of the attraction. The older generation thought they were terrible and bad. My daughter became (at the age of fifteen) a Manic Street Preachers fan and she followed them through everything they did. She bought every vinyl record they made. She's got CDs, tapes … they had a lot of bad press. They would get very drunk and it didn't seem a suitable sort of group for my daughter to be following but they have become more respectable … and I like them and I listen to their music now. I used to think it was a terrible noise – now I think they are very good. I've come round to her way of thinking!

Lin George, born 1953

It was great – there were parties and bands playing in pubs. Malvern had gigs on at the Winter Gardens, quite big bands. We used to go out to pubs a lot, to clubs, to folk clubs. I used to help at the folk club in Leigh Sinton and sing. We always seemed to be able to make entertainment. It was all fairly harmless. We used to go round to friends and play records … you were divided into two distinct camps. You were either a 'soul freak' in Worcester which meant you wore platforms and baggies or you were into rock which meant you tended to wear jeans, and to a greater or lesser degree you were or you weren't a hippie. Some people were still fairly hippie-ish. We went to see rock bands – although now they are 'middle of the road' bands you'd hear on Radio 2! Punk came along as well – I remember going to see

The Damned at Malvern. It was quite fun but not something I'd want to do a lot. I lived in jeans. I had the odd floaty skirt, floaty dresses. I had very long hair and I had an Afghan coat – and it smelt – like all Afghans do. I wish I still had it!

Sarah Blenkinsop, born 1962

Up to date with clubbing and chemicals:

I used to go out on a Friday night and the planning process starts a good week before … we sit here, look through a magazine which has got all the club listings and, 'Lets go there!' Some people have got to get new outfits, some people have to get tickets … the whole experience is you glam yourself up. You wear the most outrageous things you can think of. You wouldn't believe it. There are men dressed up as women. Women dressed up as men. People dressed up as policemen … it's a mad experience – a bit of a freak show. Then it's a mad scramble to get there. I don't like queuing up so I like to get before the big queues have started … the queues are quite interesting because you've got [people] trying to sell you tickets at twice the price, people trying to sell you drugs – you're just fending people off. The main room is usually house music – Euro-tramps' music. Then you've got two separate rooms which are drum and bass, or soul, or speed garage – I'm talking genres here – and usually it's between six and eight hours of non-stop dancing.

Gavin Yarnold, born 1976

The first thing I went to was like a hippy festival but it had rave music, acid-house music. That's where I took my first acid. There were loads of people walking round absolutely smashed out their faces on all sorts of drugs, all in colourful weird clothes, mad make-up and hair. Travellers' festivals are very open and people were shouting, 'Acid for sale,' 'Hash for sale,' or whatever. It was only £3 a tab so that's where I had my first one. It takes about three-quarters of an hour to start coming on and you realise things are not quite a normal. Things like lights and stars and things have lots of different colours and everything has trailers on it so when you see things moving fast it leaves a trail of light or a pattern after. The next stage are big raves. There were many at Castle Donnington and that's when you started taking Speed and Es then. You're looking at 20,000 people at a rave and [about] 75 per cent of them are on drugs. Speed was to keep you going all night and dancing so you didn't feel tired. You'd take Es for the ultimate sort of buzz, the rush. When they first came out, the feeling was absolutely amazing. When you were on an E you'd only have to look at somebody and you'd [feel the] warmth. It was totally emotional, rushing through your body. The music is probably designed to bring on the affects of Ecstasy. When you listen to the music the sounds … would send a sensation through your body so everything was based around Ecstasy – the whole scene.

Karen, born 1972

CHAPTER 11
Going places

Tony Baxter and her motorbike, in the
1940s.

The first ever non-slip horseshoe and travelling at 100 miles per hour. There are cars, bicycles, horse-drawn buses, plus a ferry trip across the Severn. It's a far cry from the roads at the turn of the last century, which were regarded as a safe place for the children to play. In this chapter the people of Worcestershire go places:

The streets were an ideal place for children to play because they were clean, for one thing, because the water cart came up (once, sometimes twice a week). This was a great big iron thing and there was a sprinkler at the back, and the water would sprinkle right out all over the road and these corporation men with their big bass brooms would sweep it up and down the road and wash the roadway. Of course, with horse-drawn traffic you often had manure but I never remember any being left in the road when I was a little girl because the households … would be out with their shovel and bucket to put it round the roses.

Winifred Barber, born 1907

The traffic was very, very little. There would be the occasional doctor's car, a bull nose Morris two-seater which would come up and down occasionally. There would be the motorcycles from the BSA motorcycle works and the Enfield in Redditch, and they did their testing along that road. They went as far as the old toll-house and back to test their bikes, so when they went out testing, the road wasn't ours. Otherwise, the road was our playground.

Bert Batty, born 1908

The milk float would come first in the mornings – he'd got these huge churns with his horse dragging it along. All the people down the road would put out their jugs then he'd ladle it in. Then he'd be off, then the baker would come – he had a high cart and we knew the names of all these horses and the baker was wonderful. He'd let us sit on and hold the reins and jog down the road. The children had wonderful fun. It was great. Then the fish man would come – they usually had a small horse or a pony and a big flat cart piled high with eels and a lot of them would still be wriggling because they'd still be alive. Then there'd be the knife grinder. He'd got his grinding machine and the people would be coming out of their houses with their carving knives and sometimes there'd be sparks from the wheels … we loved that. I remember a chair mender coming up the road, 'Chairs to mend, chairs to mend!' You'd see somebody-or-other lugging a chair out, putting it by their gate and he'd sit on the kerbstone and we children would sit round him watching him doing it. Everywhere was quiet. There was no aeroplanes, no wireless, no music of any kind. If you were in your house you could hear if there was anything happening in the roadway.

Winifred Barber, born 1907

Transport at that time (pre-1914) was minimal. There were buses (horse buses mark you, not motor buses) and if we wanted to go into Worcester we got on a horse bus. Two horses and the bus, open top and all that. Or there were carrier carts. We didn't use those. The villagers came in on carriers, carts,

An outing in a shooting brake, 1912.

Mondays, Wednesdays and Saturdays, the market days. The river was a gold mine for the ferry people. There were four different ferries. The charge for crossing was a penny, a halfpenny for the Strand one – he was a bit cheaper than anyone else. There were four different types: the Cathedral Ferry paddled over, the Grandstand Ferry was like a punt, the Dog and Duck Ferry had a proper boat and they rowed over in the ordinary way with two oars, and the Hallow Ferry had the same sort of boat but had one oar through the stern and they waved this and it went across. The Hallow Ferry was not very often used – it led into the Hallow Road, way up at the end, a country area. But the Dog and Duck Ferry was a very busy ferry. We knew the Dog and Duck Ferry very well. When I went to the Grammar School

I crossed over on that every day.

Richard Clay, born 1905

It was my job to take a little box truck (an old packing case with some pram wheels) push it up to the Reindeer Inn and there I had to meet carters from Martley and Broadheath who used to bring vegetables in from their farms for sale and for order and so on, and I had to collect them in my little truck and take them back to mother. Now that was the only way the produce could get into the town from the country. The farmers' wives and friends and things used to come in on the carts and do their bit of shopping while he got rid of the vegetables and eggs and butter, then they'd go back home on the cart.

Frank Wilkes, born 1904

The first Austin motor car, the Austin Seven, they put it on the road to test in 1922. I was fifteen then so I had all that childhood without any motor cars at all. I can remember one of these little Austin Sevens coming down the road. They were very, very tiny – not anything like the shape they are today. They held four! Two children in the back and a man and a woman in the front. But there were very few about. When I first went to work at Wiggins, only the boss had a car.

Winifred Barber, born 1907

When I was about five years old we lived at the Plume of Feathers which is now known as the Feathers in the Tything. We used to enjoy sitting up at the window watching the people go by. There were no motor cars about much, and if we heard one we rushed to the window to see the motor car – something most unusual. Also there were trams which used to run up and down pretty regularly every ten minutes or so and we used to like to watch that. We could see the people. They were almost level with us on the upper deck. We used to like to wave to them as they went by. Just below by the Whiteladies turning, there used to be a double line where the trams used to pass one another. They used to make a horrible noise and very often one tram got there a bit early and it had to wait until the other one came down so they could make the pass and carry on with their journeys.

Frank Wilkes, born 1904

The one most frightening time I think was being mixed up with the bicycles going to work. They'd come from all

Winifred's husband, Don Barber, with an Austin Ruby Saloon in 1939.

directions, miles away. From Astwood Bank, Alcester, Studley – all ways – all cycling to work. And when they got to the centre of the town, coming down from the south, it was a mass of cyclists and wheels. It was quite frightening to be amongst them because they were dashing for work before the eight o'clock bell went. It was a hazardous rush hour.

Bert Batty, born 1908

Coming back from Australia in the mid-1960s, Chris Cookson noticed the traffic:

T he traffic. We weren't allowed to wander round like we were in Australia. The traffic was just terrible, especially on the Stourport Road to

Tony Baxter on her hand-built racing bike, 1936.

Sarah Blenkinsop racing in July 1993 at Shelsley Walsh.

111

Kidderminster – that was a sort of block zone. You couldn't cross that road.

Chris Cookson, born 1957

The fashion became that young ladies wanted to cycle. Now, my uncle owned a big garage on the corner of Little London. He had a huge garden at the back of the garage and he had a road built around the garden and he'd got some old chap who used to teach ladies to ride their cycles round this road in the garden. I used to go over with my cousin and we used to sit in the garden and watch these ladies being taught how to ride their bikes in the garden.

Frank Wilkes, born 1904

Bert Batty's Norton 3.5horsepower combination, 1928.

The registration number was 'FK 3'. It was one of the early cars like a wagon and you had a wooden seat that you just sat in the back – three seats on the three sides. (Solid tyres, by the way.) My uncle, the one that had the garage, he took us [for] a ride one day down the A38 to Tewkesbury. We went across the river on the horse ferry in this car – came back the other road on the other side to us. This was absolutely wonderful, waving to everybody as we went by because we thought we were very important perched up on this thing going down. But it took us a whole day. If it had a bit of an incline the engine use to get hot and Uncle used to stop and we sat on the roadside while the engine cooled down and then rejoined it and went further round. It's a day that I shall remember all my life. It was most unusual and enjoyable.

Frank Wilkes, born 1904

During the war, the cars had to be put away because there was no petrol. We had to take the distribution arm out of the car and take it to the police station. They did that in case of invasion – that if the Germans arrived all these cars that were put away in the garages couldn't be used. When he took it to the police station my husband said, 'Can you tell me where it's going? What are you going to do with it?' It was part of the car and rather precious. He said, 'It's going away but I can't tell you where it's going'. I remember going with Don to get it back. There they were, all these distributor arms, dozens of them, and he looked among them and he found ours – you see of course this ticket, the same as the one we'd got, was on it. During the three years that it had been in the garage, my husband had gone down there every month and he'd turned the wheels round, he'd jacked it up and kept it all polished and cleaned and on the day that we had the distributor arm back my brother actually had a bit of petrol and he put it in the car and he said, 'Well, this is it, isn't it?' and he turned the key and it went! Absolutely wonderful. No stalling. You'd have thought he only put it in the garage an hour before.

Winifred Barber, born 1907

The first time in my life I ever did 100 miles per hour it was in a Bristol car. They used to have little opening quarter-lights for ventilation, before air conditioning or air venting or heaters were invented. If you were driving along the road with your quarter lights open they'd suddenly slam shut with a bang which frightened the life out of the drivers – particularly the aged gentleman who used to buy Bristols. And the chief engineer of Bristol came up and we went up on the Ombersley Road which was about the straightest bit of road in those days, and we did 100 miles per hour and sure enough the vents banged to, so we came back and we put stronger springs on and we went out and they didn't bang to – it was that sort of work. In basic vehicle designs we could lead the world. Even cars which we laugh at now, the A40s, were way ahead of their time for value for money and what they gave the driver. But continuous strikes and poor quality just lost our markets.

If we'd got on and worked I think we would be a very different nation.

Max Sinclair, born 1930

During the war, there was little or nothing done on the roads at all, and if the local government had got any steamrollers or anything like that, they were commandeered by the army to take across to France. It wasn't until after the end of the war, when mechanical cars and traffic and things like that were gradually increasing, that it was decided the roads had got to be repaired and there was a very big programme of intensive repairs and that was the time when surface-dressing tar and chipping started to come in, and also tarmac surfaces. Also the horses were slipping down on this new hard surface, especially on an incline when they had a heavy cart to pull, and there were many fatalities and the government decided to offer a big figure of cash to anyone who could introduce a non-slip horseshoe for these new road surfaces. Worcestershire County Council were the authority that were chosen to do this. We had these horseshoes coming in from all over the place, all over the world. This went on for some months and eventually the winner came out and I believe it was Grey's Patent Horseshoe Company from Birmingham, who placed a hard rubber insert across the frog of the shoe. But of course by the time the competition had been decided, there wasn't quite as much horse traffic on the road because cars and mechanised traffic were beginning to take over. In 1924, there were no traffic aids on the road – no traffic signals, white lines, Catseyes. The county surveyor went to America and spent some time looking at their means of traffic control. He was very impressed with some white lines they were putting down the road. We had to get the formula for painting these white lines from America because there was no paint in this country that was any use. Anyway, when the idea first came out, we couldn't really visualize how it was going to help the traffic in any way. We thought the people wouldn't take any notice of these lines. They'd never had them and they'd all wonder why they were down and wouldn't bother with them at all. But in fact the public took to them quite quickly and they were very, very successful and of course it soon developed country-wide, so Worcestershire were the pioneers of white-line painting.

After the war, the emphasis seemed to be on new roads because the traffic had developed to such an extent that the existing roads weren't capable of taking it, and this was when the government started to think of motorways. We began to design, in the late '40s, the M50. This was the second motorway to be designed and constructed in the country. The motorway was intended to take the traffic from South Wales up into the Midlands – because iron ore and so on [that] they required in the Midlands was coming up from South Wales round Port Talbot area … but by the time the M50 had been constructed, the blast furnaces were beginning to close down and although it was the second in the country, I don't think it was used to the extent that it was intended for.

Frank Wilkes, born 1904

The big changes came with the motorway. When we used to go to Cornwall before the war with my father in his Ford 8 (RD 8063 was the number!) we used to spend a week pumping up the tyres and kicking it and making sure everything was safe And it was a great expedition to go to Cornwall which took all day and half the night. Nowadays, we'd hitch up our boats and go to Helford and five hours later we're launching into the river. There are many people who say it's destruction, but for my little selfish world it's a lot of progress. I can go sailing in Helford, which I couldn't have done if it had been a long trip.

Max Sinclair, born 1930

CHAPTER 12
Life and death

A newspaper cutting of Bert in
hospital in 1926.

Bert Verity in 1940.

Visiting times in the local hospital and being admitted to the sanatorium, together with stories of childbirth then and now. People in Worcestershire talk about their experiences of childhood illness, kippers for breakfast and being 'churched' after childbirth. There are also recipes for some exciting home remedies guaranteed to bring recalcitrant children to heel:

Hospital was a frightening place to go:

About eleven years old I was when I slipped into the furnace. The doctor used to come round on a Monday so he called and said, 'Oh, hospital' – so

off I went on the bus to Worcester Hospital. My mother was with me. She leaves – that's it – you don't see anybody. It's out of the question. No visitors for children under fourteen. I felt a bit strange at first. Then you run into the routine. About ten o'clock, the matron would come round – all black, bar a little bit of white on her head, veil, gloves. Shortly after, the doctors would come round, all together. Look at your board on your bed – they may stop and look at you, they may not. Just nod their head about five minutes and gone. You had nothing to do really. You couldn't write because they had big starched sheets and you daren't mark the sheets. They had to last a week, you see. And you didn't see your own parents and you didn't know what was going on. It was nearly twelve months before I came out. I wasn't the only one. There were one or two who had been in there before me and they were still there when I came out. You could imagine what they were suffering.

Bert Verity, born 1916

Doctor Mason agreed that it was difficult for parents unable to visit their sick children:

They were sterner times. Visiting was not liberal. In my day there was always visiting. I think you've got to go to the generation before me before you get the idea of no visiting. It's very easy to look back at people and say why did they do these wicked things. But if you had come to me in 1750 with anaemia – I'd probably have bled you. Not because I was a wicked person and wanted to torture you but I'd genuinely think it was good. Certainly what they did observe was children were upset after a visit and quite peaceful in between visits. I suppose a little knowledge is a dangerous thing. I suspect it was a genuine attempt to stop suffering – but mistaken.

Bernard Mason, born 1935

I just hated walking anywhere because I had trouble. I used to come home from school (I had two miles to walk each way) and I'd get home and just curl up in the chair and cry. Dad said I was going to be given an injection. I don't think he even knew what they were going to do because they didn't discuss it those days. Dad, of course, left me and I was taken down at the end of the ward and they had one of these cut throat razors and I didn't know what they were going to do. I was just petrified. And all they done was shave my leg and paint it with iodine. I think it was the next morning – one girl had gone for an operation and she come back being violently sick but I didn't know what they'd done to her. And the next thing was I was taken and I went into a room and they'd all got their white coats on. Nurse Rice was put in charge of me and she was lovely but I just held me breath 'cos they put a mask over me face and I just held me breath because I was petrified. Utterly petrified I was. And when I came round I felt sick and my foot was stuck up on a pillow or something and every time it gradually sank down and they'd come up and shake it up again and put it higher. I couldn't eat. They brought me kippers for breakfast and the one nurse

said, 'How long are you going to be here?' and I said 'Three days.' And she said, 'Well if you'd have been here longer my girl I'd have made you eat it'.

Mary Beattie, born 1929

Mary contracted scarlet fever:

I can remember having this terrible, terrible sore throat. It was 1935 and I was six years old. Of course in those days you didn't really send for the doctor, especially not at the weekend. Anyway, this went on over the weekend and they discovered it was scarlet fever which was quite a serious illness and the

Mary Beattie in Priory Park, Great Malvern, 1932.

Mary Beattie, c. 1930s.

isolated and every day you had to have a bath in a sort of yellow liquid. I don't know whether it was sulphur or what – I hated those because you smelt all day. I hate that smell.

Mary Beattie, born 1921

Harriet had her own remedies to keep her healthy:

I always believe in the old remedies. If you had pneumonia, or a cold [we used to use elderflower blossom] you'd get that, hang it up in a net and let it dry and you'd boil it like tea, put it in a saucepan, strain it through a tea strainer and you'd sup it. That would clear your infected chest. Not like these cranky drugs today. And there used to be another remedy we'd get. They called it liquid fruit and you'd get a teaspoonful. It was lovely. It'd burn you right down from the top of your throat right down to the bottom of your stomach! And you'd turn round and say, 'Look, I'm better this morning'. If you'd have had a spoonful of that you'd have been up on your feet!

Harriet Hall, born 1922

We took my son into the hospital. That was '56 and I was horrified we weren't allowed to visit and I couldn't understand why and I asked and they said nobody was allowed to visit because they deemed it would unsettle them. That was a terrible thing and it seemed a very long week to me, so what it felt like to him I do not know and it certainly made an

next thing I can remember I was being carted off in an ambulance to the isolation hospital which is in Half Key Road. It was absolutely pouring with rain and nobody had told me what was going on. I was just so terrified. I wasn't sure whether I'd done something terrible or what. Anyway, I got to the isolation hospital and it was a grim looking place and I was the only child in there for six weeks and really didn't understand what was going on because nobody explained anything to you. Mum used to come down on her bike to see me but she wasn't allowed in. We used to look at each other through the window. That six weeks seemed like forever. I remember feeling very lonely and impression on him because he was quite odd for a week or so. He was upstairs in his room and he'd call me up – he'd say, 'Mum' and I'd go running up and he'd say, 'Go away I hate you' and put his head under the sheet. It had quite a bad effect on him.

Mary Beattie, born 1929

Back in the late '40s, early '50s they made a famous film of the children in hospital basically showing [that] yes, the children are more malleable in the ward when they don't see their parents but it's because they are depressed. And this film showed it in no uncertain terms and it caused an uproar. There was a lovely old chap – he went to see the film with his ward Sister and he said, 'What do you think Sister?' And she said, 'I'm totally convinced' and he said, 'I'm not sure' and she said a few words and apparently next morning he said, 'Let them in' so as far as I can see, the first full visiting started then. I can remember in the late '70s or early '80s going around the ward and for a nominal twenty-four kids we had nearly seventy bodies in that room. Now that may be getting over the top. I don't know.

Bernard Mason, born 1935

Mary Beattie had her baby early, then a quick sit down and a cigarette with the midwife:

Ronkswood was still a military hospital then and there were no maternity hospitals around. So, when

The Malvern Cowleigh Church Mother Union, 1920s.

you were having a baby you either paid to go to a nursing hospital if you could afford it or you had your baby at home. Well I couldn't afford it, so my son was born at home. Unfortunately he was premature so he spent his first night in a chest of drawers drawer with a blanket. And the midwife came back the next morning and she said, 'Oh, you have been a good girl' because she'd come down on her bike not thinking the baby was born and she hadn't brought her black bag, so she had nothing to help me with the labour and the birth and she said, 'Oh, you have been a good girl. You can have a nice cup of tea now'. And I said, 'That would be nice – and I wouldn't half like a cigarette!' And she said, 'So would I – we'll have one together' and so she sat on the bed and we had a cup of tea and a cigarette because smoking wasn't frowned on then like it is today!

Mary Beattie, born 1929

When you go back to the turn if the century, what you've got is delicate babies [that] were looked after by superb nursing or they died. And the usual thing was you'd wrap them in cotton wool and put them in a shoe box near the fire. If they went, they went. If they didn't, they didn't. In my early days in Intensive Care, I've had some children brought in who spent the first twelve hours by the fire. By the '40s, we'd got to the idea of thermostats to keep them warm, and feeding tubes. We were still before antibiotics. The end of the '50s, things were really moving because ventilators and monitors were beginning to come

in and one was beginning to be able to breathe for children who couldn't breathe for themselves.

Bernard Mason, born 1935

The churching of women was still practised:

On the Monday, the midwife came in and she wasn't very happy with my son, and I wasn't either. He was four and a half pounds born – and the whole of Sunday night he'd cried. And she said, 'I'm sorry but baby's quite poorly and he's got to go to the hospital. The ambulance will be here in a minute but have you decided on a name?' And I said, 'Yes, Alec'. So she said, 'We're going to baptise baby before he goes'. And I thought, 'Oh dear, that sounds a bit frightening'. Anyway, the ambulance came and my husband was still on leave and he went in the ambulance with our son and they went to the Lucy Baldwin Hospital in Stourport, which is a long way. The following Friday I said, 'Look – I've just got to go and see my baby'. So, in those days as well, you had to be churched before you could go anywhere and it was the vicar who married us and he said, 'You know why you've come don't you Mary?' I said, 'Yes, you've come to thank God it's over!' And he looked at my husband and he said, 'And you've come to thank God you didn't have to go through it!' He was delightful! So I got churched and on the Saturday we decided to go to see the baby, and we walked down to the Link, the Malvern Link, and got a bus there to Worcester.

[We] had to change buses at Worcester, get a bus to Stourport and it was about a two mile walk to the hospital (this was just after I'd been confined) And we said, 'We've come to see baby Beattie' and she [the nurse] said, 'Right, don't get too close and don't touch him and you can have two minutes!' And it was two minutes and off we had to go! I can remember crying all the way home.

Mary Beattie, born 1929

Having a baby at forty was considered a great risk to take:

As I was forty the nurse came round and said I'd better go into a maternity unit. I said, 'Alright then'. It was a bad start. It was a very old nursing home and she said, 'Why didn't you ring to let us know you were coming?' Well, there were no phones – my husband had had to cycle to the phone. And she said, 'If nothing happens, you go back home'. I thought, 'Very nice'. And I was put in a bed and I was having terrible pain. I was really in labour and I could tell the baby was going to arrive and I shouted, 'Will you fetch the nurse please!' They were down the other end. It was a long corridor. And nothing happened. Nobody came past. The baby arrived in bed. And I'd gone in to be looked after. I shouted,'Will you tell the nurses my baby's arrived!' They all rushed in and they took the baby and I didn't see her till six o'clock at night. Terrible. Talk about bonding – the others at home were put into your arms as soon as they'd been born, before they washed them. Well, I thought it had died or

there was something wrong … I thought, 'They don't want to tell me!' Well, I lay all day. Six o'clock came and the nurse came in with three babies and she said, 'Which is yours?' and I said, 'That one' and she said, 'There you are then'. And I said, 'Oh, haven't you got big feet – and your hands'. And she came back to me and said, 'Come on back to the nursery if your mother's going to pick flies with you'. And she took her back!

Lilly Peach, born 1920

Modern hospitals might have been less stern but it was still an uncomfortable experience for Lin George:

I had to have an epidural because my blood pressure being so high – they thought they would keep my blood pressure low. So I'd got a needle and a tube going into my spine. I'd got a drip going into my arm from where they'd induced labour and then I'd got this plate which was attached to the baby's head which was then connected. Well, it looked rather like an incubator-sized piece of machinery on this trolley which had all these different read-outs monitoring the baby's heartbeat. I couldn't move comfortably because I was anchored by wires at three different points in my body and it wasn't very pleasant but I did feel I was really being taken care of and having the best attention possible. In fact, when Simon was born he was quite blue – I think he had got quite distressed. He didn't breathe initially. He didn't make a sound and they rushed him over to the corner of the room and I couldn't see what was going on – and then a minute later he started to cry and he was fine then. That was a bit worrying because for a little while I wasn't sure if he'd made it.

Lin George, born 1953

Kath Robinson looks back on having her first baby in 1953:

We simply had to do what we were told! We didn't have much choice. I had a very good doctor and I got on well with him, but we weren't prepared for what was going to happen. I don't think we knew what was going to happen. We just went along with what they said. I went into the nursing home to have her and I was left alone for about four hours, which was dreadful – all through the night. Then she was born at twelve o'clock the next day and I remember bringing her home and feeling very nervous. I was sick before I had her and I remember the nurse coming in and saying, 'Oh, don't worry about that. It's a sign of safe labour!

Kathleen Robinson, born 1929

The last word is from Jane on the birth of her baby:

For the first twenty-four hours I was ecstatic. I was on cloud nine. Nobody could have done anything to change that feeling. I just literally stared at him for twenty-four hours thinking, 'He's mine, he's mine!' Then I had a few problems with breast feeding and I started to panic a little bit. He didn't feed properly for the first couple of days. He didn't seem to know what to do. He did cry quite a bit and I was exhausted after a couple of days. I hadn't had any sleep. So they did take him down to their nursery unit and looked after him for a few hours so I could get some sleep but I didn't sleep. It didn't feel right. All of a sudden I was a mother and my baby wasn't there. When my mum was in hospital the babies were brought to the mums to be fed and taken away again. I think it was every four hours regardless of whether they cried or not. Well today, it's demand feeding … I think Ben was feeding off me for twenty-four hours one day. It's much more liberal now in hospital and you can do much more. The National Childbirth Trust has had a lot to do with that. They've worked very hard to give women more choices in hospital. My mum was in hospital for a lot longer. I was in hospital for a week but that was because I'd had a Caesarean. There were women coming in who'd had normal deliveries and were gone a few hours later and that seems incredible. With my mum, she had three normal deliveries – she was in for a week or even ten days. So obviously the length of time you are in hospital has changed quite a bit. I was made to feel very important. They always came when I asked. They were very supportive, they always had time for me. It was the most amazing experience ever!

Jane Williams, born 1968

CHAPTER 13
Beliefs and fears

Derrick Bollen in 1926.

The people of Worcestershire discuss their religious beliefs, from the hard task of becoming a Catholic, the geranium theory, and discovering God in a local park:

In the First World War, I could not understand how both sides could pray to the same God for victory – both sides thinking their sides were right. It just didn't mean anything. I shall never forget the attitude of the Church to life. They were recruiting people to go to the killing fields. The Church was so outdated. Even after the war, it was outdated.

Robert Bell, born 1911

On Sundays, the upper class went in the morning and they had their select seats in the church. In the evening, the rest of the village went to church with the children, mostly women. It was accepted – semi-mediaeval, if you like, The well-educated people really ran the village. They formed the nucleus of the Parish Council. The vicar was a powerful influence in the village on the young people. When I was a young boy that particular vicar preached hellfire. He was one of the old-fashioned ones. Later, with the more benevolent attitude on the part of the clergy, things improved. I think there's a good rapport between the village and the clergy.

Richard Clay, born 1905

What turned me against God was the Holocaust in the Second World War. I had been a believer and been brought up to be a good Christian, and we were all taught about almighty God. We really didn't know until the end of the war about the Holocaust, and for the first time for a long time I went

Bert Batty (back row, third from the right) and his bible class in the 1920s.

Jim Beechey's choir.

to church with my family, to Tardebigge church. The sermon was about the slaughter of the first-born and it hit me – if there is a God, what was he doing about the slaughter of the first-born, and then what was he doing about the Jews. There's nobody up there. It's absolutely patent to me. It's just a myth that has been brought about by evangelists.

It's wrong to say I've abandoned religion. There is a belief in me that if we had the religion that we had when I was a growing child ... it was so good for us that we learned right from wrong, we learned it in a good way. It is still essential, I believe, that we should not abandon church-going. It is good for us. It helps us to be straight, honest people.

Bert Batty, born 1908

Freda Dutton has developed her own theory:

There's no afterlife. There's no greater being. We are here, we die and that's the end, and the thing that is most important is the world around us and human beings. My philosophy isn't baptism or Christianity or Hinduism. It's called the 'geranium syndrome'. If you've ever kept geraniums you know that they go along, throwing out their leaves, they're quite happy, and you stop the water – they go dry and they panic and they think, 'We've got to create the next generation – we're on the way out!' So they throw up their flowers, they grow out their seeds and that's okay. The next generation is catered for. That, I think, happens to everything and everybody and I think with human beings, with animals, the most important force is the sexual force. The most important thing is getting the next generation. Cunningly disguised. It feels nice, it's great fun, but the most important thing is that you are getting the next generation along. So yes, okay. It's humanism and my geranium syndrome!

Freda Dutton, born 1932

When I came to this country, and wasn't under the influence of my parents anymore, twice a year I definitely went to church – Christmas and Easter. I suppose for years I went on. I had everything. I had a lovely home, a husband who loved me and I loved him. I had this baby who was like having a doll. She was as good as gold and yet there was something missing and I didn't know what it was. One night I'd gone to midnight service, Christmas Eve, and I came out thinking, 'Yes! That wonderful feeling during the service, this warmth within me'. And I was walking back through the local park and it must have been kids … they'd put a tripwire across the path and I fell over it and instinctively I cursed – and instantly that feeling was gone. And I can remember getting up and thinking yes, I'd been annoyed I'd fallen but what hurt me more was that feeling had gone. I perhaps drifted in a way for a couple more years but I never forgot that feeling I'd had. Looking back, it was God opening my heart and saying, 'Just come!' But it took a couple more years for me to finally make that move and I was glad I did because my life now – I can see purpose in my life now. I try to live … the way the Lord would like me to live. I try to do everything with that in

mind. I know I've got a long way to go but I'm on the road.

Mary Macdiarmid, born 1948

Sue Nixon gradually moved towards the Catholic faith over a period of years, but found it was harder to be accepted into the faith than she anticipated:

When I became a weekly boarder I changed … to the Convent and I actually considered being a nun. I think the nuns always thought I would. I didn't sleep with the others – I had a room in the nuns' quarters. Looking back, I think they were giving me space to test if that was what I wanted to do. If there was ever a visiting priest it was always me who was sent to have tea with them – just in case I might like to talk to him. They never openly raised the subject. They never pressurised me at all and I wasn't even a Catholic at the time. I thought about it after I first went to London and I started a course of instruction. In those days, if you became a Catholic you could never attend a church of another denomination and I just couldn't reconcile that as being Christian. To say I would never go to church with my father again was something I couldn't possibly do so I cut. I left it at that. I didn't go any further. Then I moved flats and there was a Catholic church down the road and I started to go and then I met Malcolm. He actually came from an Irish-Protestant background and he was terrified of the Catholic church but I suppose, looking back, he was also terrified of losing me so he came with me and we enjoyed it hugely. It was just after the Vatican Council – it was in English, there was folk singing, there were guitars and in fact when we got married I was actually married from the Convent and at the end we had a service called Benediction and Blessing in the Convent Chapel before we left. It was a great influence on our lives. The Church of England, we felt, had lost its way. Euthanasia and abortion were being discussed at great length because the Abortion Act had just come in. We had all been told, 'Thou shalt not kill'. It was unequivocal. There may be steps within it but that had to be stated and for us we didn't feel the Church of England were getting their act together and that made us veer towards the Catholic Church. We approached the priest here. He started to instruct – in the meantime my father was becoming less well. He was very interested in the Catholic Church as well and we were all instructed together and my father was due to be received into the church first because of his ill health and he rang his brother and his brother was very condemning and he backed off. He said, 'I'm not going to hurt my brother' and everything went on ice. When we came back after my father had died, the church were very slow. They felt we shouldn't 'bounce' into anything. We felt we'd been at it for years. 'Come on! Let us in!' The Catholic Church felt we should wait, and the priest said, 'Now go away for six months. I don't want to see you. And if you still want to be received into the church, you can come back'. We felt enormously frustrated. We wanted to get in. We were shut on the outside. There was nothing we could do so we had to go away for anther six

months and then finally they said yes and we were received into the church at Easter which was a deeply spiritual experience. We'd reasoned it all out academically – we were going ahead doing something. We didn't expect this enormous kick that we were going to get out of it. We were on a high for a very long time and I think I will always fight back [against] people who say the Catholic Church are grabbing at souls and they don't believe in contraception – they want more Catholics. You should try getting in there. It definitely isn't true!

Sue Nixon, born 1946

I grew up in a very conservative church-based community. I got forced to go to church and hated it … sitting still … sitting in these rock-hard wooden pews listening to this chap rant on and you'd be counting the coloured panes in the glass and if you started to fidget you'd be told, 'When I get you home my boy, you're in for a thrashing!' All this sort of stuff and it was awful. But there was this youth group started in the church and I got quite involved and, to cut a long story short, got into it. I think the youth group wanted to see themselves as slightly more at the cutting edge, slightly more evangelical. It led onto me going off to Africa for a year with the Presbyterian Church of Ireland. I would never have said I was a missionary or anything like that but certainly they sent me out and gave me a small allowance, and I went out with a chap who was a missionary and we went to an agricultural community development at the foot of Mount Kenya. Where we were, there was only the Presbyterian Church which was why we were there out in the bush, but in other areas you would tend to find Methodist churches next door to Anglican churches, next door to Catholic churches. And they all seemed to be in competition with each other out there saying, 'If you come to our church, your kids can be treated freely in our clinic,' 'If you come to our church your kids can come freely to our school,' and I thought, 'Hold on a minute. This isn't too hopeful here'. Fascinating though. Come November when it was circumcision time for the girls, which is illegal still but very, very much part of the culture, you began to wonder just how deep the success of this Christian planting had been because the old customs still spoke loudly. Anyway, it was a real eye-opening year – a superb experience and I'm very pleased to have been given that but certainly not a year where you could come away unchallenged. I came back, went to Sheffield, immediately joined the Christian Fellowship, became a bigwig in that, but let's just say after a couple of years, it stopped. It collapsed. I don't know why. I started to recognise it wasn't really what I felt. I was very damaged by the Church, I feel, when I looked back, when I started fundamentally questioning my own beliefs – feeling that very much it was guilt-based religion. Yet the phraseology, the wording and the concepts were full of liberation, full of love, full of forgiveness and yet my experience was there's this God up there looking down and if you transgress somewhere, 'Bad boy. Don't do it again' and you'd just be wracked with guilt. I felt very disappointed and I then started to explore things like Quakerism which were much more contemplative – much less shouting and banging on about things, much more looking within, being quiet. Most Christians, especially where I come from and the sort I used to be, are black and white and when you've got no space for doubt or grey or recognising that maybe you don't have all the answers, I'm very wary of that. I think there are many questions in life and as soon as one individual or one group starts to say, 'Actually we have the answer to life and we know and … we're going to sell it to you', be you a missionary in Africa, or be you in the streets of Kidderminster, I immediately turn off. The answer to life is unknown and I feel that makes us much more humble and much more accepting of other people. I now live quietly for myself, I don't really look for any answers. I don't want to harm anyone. I don't want to hurt anything. You could see parallels with the whole environmental thing, and sometimes when I'm talking to a group of students about the environmental damage we have done and how we have an opportunity to do something different there I think, 'Well, I could be talking about religion here in a way' – so I sometimes stop myself and hold back.

Iain Patton, born 1966